CAMINO ENCOUNTERS

Pauline McNulty

Published 2019 by Pauline McNulty

poilinmcnulty@gmail.com

ISBN 978-1-5272-3540-3

Designed by Vizz Creative, www.vizz.biz

Printed by GPS Colour Graphics Ltd, Belfast

Cover Illustration: Navarre Dreaming

All illustrations/photographs and poems are the work of the author

PREFACE

I don't know when I first thought of walking the Camino de Santiago, or how I heard about it – it was just always there, something I knew I would be doing, sometime.

When I finally did get around to it, I fell totally under its spell, and I wanted to share it with everyone on the planet, whether they wanted to hear about it or not. So, I tried writing a novel about it, which I abandoned, then I wrote poems and painted pictures, but I was not satisfied with them, either. After many attempts, I arrived at last at this point, the beginning of the story of my personal walk on the Camino de Santiago de Compostela.

This book is not written in chronological order, it is simply a collection of memories of people and places I encountered on the way. While the people and events may seem improbable, they are indeed all very real and the events surrounding them are exactly as they happened. I kept diaries and filled several notebooks, but even without those, the sounds, sights and smells are lodged in my memory. It's all there in my head and I can call it up instantly. From the scent of dry earth on a furnace-hot day on the meseta, yellow dust rising from each step, to the sounds of an orchestra playing in the streets of Santiago, I will never forget.

I have not used the names of those I met or travelled with, in order to protect their own personal pilgrimage.

Albergue - Hostal

Peregrino - Pilgrim

Sello - Stamp

Dedicated to my family, first in my heart, as always.

CONTENTS

CAMINO ENCOUNTERS

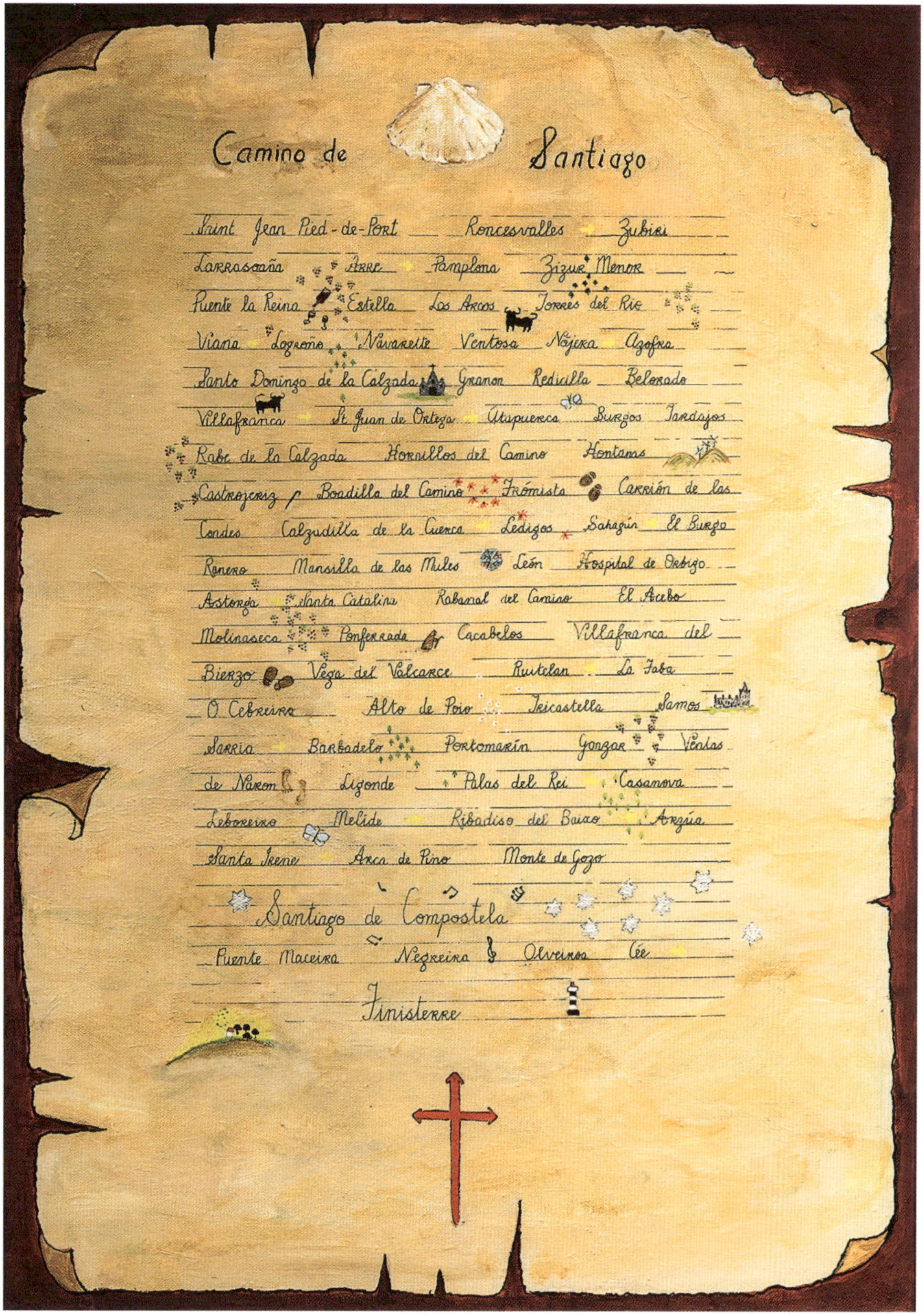
Camino de Santiago
Saint Jean Pied-de-Port Roncesvalles Zubiri
Larrasoaña Arre Pamplona Zizur Menor
Puente la Reina Estella Los Arcos Torres del Rio
Viana Logroño Navarrete Ventosa Nájera Azofra
Santo Domingo de la Calzada Granon Redicilla Belorado
Villafranca St Juan de Ortega Atapuerca Burgos Tardajos
Rabe de la Calzada Hornillos del Camino Hontanas
Castrojeriz Boadilla del Camino Frómista Carrión de las
Condes Calzadilla de la Cueza Ledigos Sahagún El Burgo
Ranero Mansilla de las Mulas León Hospital de Orbigo
Astorga Santa Catalina Rabanal del Camino El Acebo
Molinaseca Ponferrada Cacabelos Villafranca del
Bierzo Vega del Valcarce Ruitelan La Faba
O. Cebreira Alto de Poio Tricastella Samos
Sarria Barbadelo Portomarín Gonzar Ventas
de Naron Ligonde Palas del Rei Casanova
Leboreiro Melide Ribadiso del Baixo Arzúa
Santa Irene Arca de Pino Monte de Gozo
Santiago de Compostela
Puente Maceira Negreira Olveiroa Cée
Finisterre

Camiño
de
Santiago

PART 1

ST. JEAN PIED DE PORT TO RONCESVALLES.

It is hot, so hot. I lie on my bunk in 55 rue de la Citadel, sticky and uncomfortable. It's 3am, and I am desperate for sleep, knowing the next day – my first day on the Camino – will be long and difficult. The dormitory is full, the door and single window wide open, but the air is thick as treacle, and sleep will not come. I contemplate going out to the neglected garden at the back of the building to cool off in the night air, but it had taken a considerable amount of effort to get up into my bunk bed, and I quail at the thought of scrambling around in the semi-dark, disturbing those blessed with sleep. I twist and turn, listening to sighs and snores, resigned to sleeplessness. I close my eyes, trying to force myself to settle but it's useless.

In spite of myself, my weary eyes open. I find myself looking straight into the unwavering stare of the occupant of the upper bunk level with mine. His dark grey eyes hold their steady gaze, less than three feet separating the bunk beds. He is young, perhaps seventeen or eighteen, and I gradually become aware that he is unable to turn away, or get down from his bed, as he is handcuffed to the bed. A chain runs down to the man below, wrapped arround and locked to the man's wrist.

Oh.

Bizarrely, I then fall into a deep slumber. Do I dream that I hear their whispered voices later in the night, the sound of rucksacks being packed, boots laced up? Maybe, but when I wake, there is no sign of them, their rucksacks, boots and chains – all gone. I never see them again.

I hear rustling, water running, then someone switches on the light. Most of the beds are empty, and that's when I realise I should be gone too. I slide down from my perch, taking a handful of clothes with me. Soon, I am packed, clothed and booted. I am last to leave. I look again at that bunk – did I dream that? I dither about on the dark cobbled street – refilling my water bottle, re-tying my laces, hoping some other pilgrim will come past who I can tag along behind. Nobody comes. I don't like walking in the dark. Should have thought of that sooner.

"Oh, for heaven's sake!" I say to myself, "Just get on with it!"

There is nothing left to do, except to start walking. One foot in front of the other, left, right, left, right, on and on – and up and up. Up starts immediately, no gentle introduction, and it keeps going on, relentless. I feel a little bit vulnerable, a lone female in the dark. Gradually, light steals into the sky and I see other pilgrims ahead, tiny plodding figures in the distance. I stop from time to time, turning slowly in a 360-degree circle, taking in the incredible landscape that surrounds me. Deep valleys running down to where tiny villages nestle in the folds of the earth, red roofs, white walls, now far below me. Forests marching up the sides of verdant slopes, as though they sought to match their stride with mine. On the higher slopes, sheep nibble daintily, under a sky so wide, so blue, that I realise that I am crying, and everywhere the sound of cowbells ringing gently.

Other pilgrims pass me, with a heartfelt 'Buen Camino!', and occasionally – just occasionally – I manage to pass those who are actually slower than me. But this is not a race. Around midday, I let myself sink onto the warm, dusty earth, the short stubby grass, pulling out a soggy tomato baguette, and attacking it as though I haven't eaten for a week. I study the route, which I photocopied before I left home, with the intention of discarding each piece as I completed it, to save weight, but I have used the back of the page to make some notes, so I replace them carefully. (They are before me now as I write, crumpled but legible.) It's time to move on, still a long way to go. I try to stand up, but my legs are like jelly and it takes a few moments to feel some strength come back in to them. I blame the unceasing ascent, and proceed carefully for the next few kilometres.

From time to time, I notice Griffon vultures circling slowly below me, riding on the thermals, emphasizing the height I've reached. With a wingspan of up to 3 metres, they are the biggest birds that I have ever seen, and it seems that I am almost close enough to touch them. But suddenly I realise that now they are almost overhead, and oh bliss, I am going down at last! The majestic birds are now just where they should be – high above me. A steep grassy slope lies before me and it is surprising how difficult it is to descend; the grass is slippery and my legs have forgotten how to go downhill. Now I begin to catch up with other pilgrims, as we stumble on rubbery legs down to where the Camino briefly meets a tarmac road. At last, I arrive at a shrine and a tiny chapel, probably the smallest in Spain, and I hear voices singing a familiar hymn, but in German. There is no room for more than a dozen people inside, so I stand at the back and join in, crushed comfortably between two handsome Italian pilgrims. Our voices in our different languages soar together, and when the song is ended, there are tears and smiles as we wish on another 'Buen Camino!'.

I pick up my walking stick, and prepare to leave, when a lady catches my arm, talking excitedly, leading me around the other side of the building, but I speak no German and she speaks no English, so I try to pull away. Oh, but then I see a huge white tour bus, and from it the German contingent are busy bringing food to load onto two long trestle tables. At least, to one of the tables – the other holds numerous bottles of wine, and glasses aplenty. The food is amazing, breads, cheeses, salads, meats of every kind, and we, the pilgrims just passing by, are invited to share the bounty. In broken English, it is explained that these people are making a peace and reconciliation tour along part of the Camino route, half from east Berlin, half from west Berlin. It is very important to them to meet and share their journey with others, and this is their first day on their mission. A glass is pressed into my hand, to be refilled time and again, and in the surreal surroundings of a small lay-by on a remote mountain road, I proceed to get quietly drunk.

Midafternoon finds me comfortably leaning back against a wall, my feet stretched out before me, and a wine glass still in my hand. Empty. However, there is still a couple of kilometres to go, so I rouse myself from my torpor and stagger to my feet. One of the handsome Italians helps me with my rucksack, and after saying goodbye to my hosts, I am off again. The route now plunges steeply down, down through light dappled woodland and at first, my feet don't quite fall where I want them to. I weave about, singing lustily, until a few scary stumbles on tree roots which could have sent me cart wheeling into space sobers me up. I take things carefully, and as I am picking my way daintily along, two young girls of perhaps eighteen or nineteen year pass me. They are wearing pale blue dresses and head scarves which I recognise as the garments for novice nuns. They are giggling and laughing and singing all at once, running lightly down the path. Far below can be seen buildings and people like tiny dots, though they are getting clearer with each step. In a graveled courtyard the tiny figure of a small, round, elderly nun paces slowly back and forth, arms folded in the ample sleeves of her black habit.

As they enter the courtyard, the young girls call out excitedly. The old nun looks up, a beaming smile on her face, as she opens her arms like welcoming wings, and they fling themselves into her loving embrace. Linking arms, they move slowly to a door in the courtyard wall and pass from my sight, their laughter an echo of love on the sweet evening air.

Under the high vaulted ceiling of a converted monastery, I am snuggled cosily in my sleeping bag. Curfew is at 10.00 pm, when the lights go out and the door is shut. To maximise space, the bunks are pushed together, so I am in what is, essentially, a double bed. I am too tired to care. A tiny French man occupies the space beside me, and we have placed our rucksacks chastely in a line between us. He is weeping quietly, as his wife and two small children have earlier said goodbye. They had motored from Perpignion to Roncesavalles to make sure he had safely crossed the Pyrenees, but are now on their way home. He is wearing a tee-shirt with the children's names printed on it. I hope he is not going to cry all night.

Promptly at 10.00 pm, the lights go out. I hear much muttering, fiddling with zips and occasional muffled laughter, until at last, all 200 beds are quiet – for a while. Then the snorers begin, and every note on the snorer scale is played, accompanied by nasal whistling exhalations, the high ceiling encouraging amplification. After a while,

I grow accustomed to the sounds, and I am about to topple into the deep soft dark of slumber, when there is an almighty crash of thunder. Bolts of lightning stab the dark with fierce white light, and I sit up in alarm, bumping my head on the bunk above me. Uttering a few profanities, I fall grumpily asleep.

4.00 am. My kidneys are awake, demanding immediate relief. It is pitch dark, the toilets are a long way down a flight of steps and I can't find my torch. Then oh, what luck! A pale shape, which looks like a lady in a nightgown drifts by, presumably on the same errand. I slither out of my sleeping bag and follow, but on reaching the steps she has vanished. There is nothing I can do but carry on, and at last I come up from the dark bowels of the earth, mission accomplished. Oh heck – where is my bunk? I have no idea how far along the wall it is, I only know its on the left – or is it the right – bottom tier. I dither for a few cold minutes, then I remember I draped my wet socks over the end of my bunk, beside the small Frenchman's, so I shuffle along, feeling the bottom of each bunk, muttering 'four wet socks, four wet socks' like a mantra. Finally, I find four wads of sodden wool, and before I can agonise further, I dive into the bunk, praying it's empty. Yes, it is, and I fall back, instantly asleep. Good night.

Part Two

ZUBIRI

This dry river bed is endless. I slip and slide over slate that sits at an angle, razor sharp. Just one fall would be enough to cause serious damage, so I pick my way carefully. Others pass me, romping confidently by, or waiting patiently where there is no room as I proceed at snail's pace. As I walk, I scan the vegetation along the banks of the river for anything of interest, the habit of a lifetime. One of my friends once told me that I had 'an eye in my head like a travellin rat'. I stop to tie my laces a little tighter, and as I stoop over, a small movement catches my eye. It's a butterfly, probably a small tortoiseshell. I lean nearer, careful not to let my shadow cause it to flutter away. No, it's not a small tortoiseshell, it's a comma! I've never seen one before, except in books, how exciting!

"Hey, look! Here's a comma butterfly – look at the lovely shape of him".

I am shouting, but no-one seems to be interested, they just plod on by this crazy Irish woman, watching their feet on the treacherous ground.

"Don't stop, for God's sake, you might see something wonderful!" I am shrieking now, but it appears that they do not speak English. Ah well. The butterfly obligingly waits, posing prettily when I manage to extricate my camera from my rucksack. I finally get the photo, without even asking his permission.

Late afternoon and I cross the small bridge into Zubiri, wander slowly to the albergue which is fortunately close by. I take off my boots, then peel off my socks and stand in the short queue on the cool concrete steps leading inside. My feet are delighted. It is taking forever to advance, the lady at a small table deliberating over every detail of passports, pilgrim passports, determined to unearth any proof that one could have cheated and got a bus. When it's nearly my turn, she stands up abruptly. She gathers up her papers, and hangs a sign on the door.

"COMPLETO"

What? I don't believe it, I just don't believe it. We, the dispossessed, mill about aimlessly, thinking of the 6kms to the next albergue, with no guarantee that it won't be full too. I also think of trying to put my boots back on over sticky, sweaty socks, and toes newly released from the restriction of boots are never too happy about that, either.

Then, a saviour appears, a small grumpy man who indicates that we should follow him through a gate in the high wire fence that surrounds the albergue. Someone mutters 'Colditz', the man stops and stares severely at the eager throng following him, all trying to look innocent. 'It wasn't me, sir' written all over their faces. He leads us to a huge, partially built sports hall, one wall of which is made of packing boxes piled carelessly in a cascade of cardboard. About 50 bunks sit forlornly in the middle of the vast space, no sheets, no pillows, just a thin mattress on most – the rest had nothing but the wire base. I quickly claim a lower bunk, and sort through my gear, getting ready to have a shower.

The good news is that there is a shower, the bad news is that there are two showers and two toilets – to serve over a hundred people. And, they are in a mobile unit in the street! On the pavement, actually, and the queue is a long one. I finally get to my turn, I see the queue for the toilet is a separate one, and I have no choice, I must yield to my kidneys once again. Finally, I reach the shower. These facilities are of a temporary nature, and of flimsy construction, the door merely a half of what is generally usual, so from my knee down is visible to all and sundry, and from my shoulders up are also. I could have a conversation with any passer-by while attending to the necessities, should I wish to do so. And the water is cold, of course.

By now, it is almost 8 o'clock, so I join a group of pilgrims who have discovered the only restaurant that is open. The food is good, and the convivial atmosphere restores us. We wander back to the albergue, just in time to welcome an elderly Japanese man with a burst of cheers and applause. He started at dawn, and it has taken him an incredible thirteen hours to get here. He is shyly thankful for the warmth of his welcome, and he is plied with food, then escorted to a comfortable bunk by someone who gives up their claim to it. Curfew doesn't seem to apply here, as someone produces a guitar, another a tambourine, and we dance and sing until nearly midnight, around a bonfire glowing and sparking.

Zubiri is not finished with us just yet. As the straggling line of pilgrims leave next morning, one by one we find a state-of-the-art leisure centre about three hundred yards away, on the edge of this small town. The sauna, steam room, swimming pool and Jacuzzi had been available for anyone yesterday, opening hours nine am. To nine pm. Zubiri, you win.

PART THREE

WHY?

When you are in the middle of something, do you ever find yourself wondering why you are doing it? Quite often, there is no particular answer. I am reflecting on my reasons for doing the Camino, and I can't remember ever deciding, the thought was just always there. I had an inflated idea of the depth of my beliefs, and it seemed a grand idea, a holy gesture. I began a diary in the days leading up to the start of my walk, with the intention of making many profound and life-changing observations, which I could after bestow upon anyone who had the misfortune to cross my path.

In this diary there is a page with 'why'? written in huge letters. Back then, when I knew everything and was always right, I felt confident enough to make fun of the questions which such remarks as 'I think I will look good in a coarse woollen tunic and good quality sandals' or to hope 'It is enough for Him to give me the nod when I reach the pearly gates'.

Then, pompously, 'To glorify God' or 'To become more holy in His sight'. Finally, 'For a lovely long walk'

In hindsight, I really had no idea, I just wanted to go. Then life moved the goal posts. I got my second bout of cancer, and that changed everything. Whether I was sick due to chemotherapy, or missing my children while in hospital or throwing up in secret so as not to distress my family, God felt so close to me that my happiness in His constant presence left no room for fear.

Then I got better.

The support from the chemotherapy team, the weekly trips to the hospital all ceased, and I was alone. It was no longer necessary to be so closely watched, and I found that scary. 'What if it comes back?' was always in the back of my mind. I lost that closeness, that constant knowing He was with me. I felt that even He had stepped back too, leaving me on my own. Where was He?

I wanted to beg Him to be close to me again, but I was afraid. Afraid it would mean that getting cancer or some other affliction was the only way to be able to have that love. Sometimes I wanted the courage to say "Okay, God, give me cancer again, so that I can know You again." But I never did.

One day, just an ordinary day before I left to walk the Camino, I knew, I suddenly knew why I needed to.

It was perfectly simple.

I just needed to be alone with Him.

LOSING YOU.

If it had been just
You and me –
but everyone
thought I was either
daft or saved.
Everyone gave their opinion
on how I should love You
or not.
So I let go. And now
I live alone.

But my times are
In Your hands,
and I will know You
again.

This time, it will be
different.

I will hold You in my heart
secret
and tell no-one.

PART FOUR

PAMPLONA IS MAGIC.

I am exhausted. I follow the high circular wall that surrounds the ancient city of Pamplona, heat emanating from the dressed stones, making me gasp for air. I keep going, round the circle, surely I must be near a gate or a door. A wave of thick, burning air washes over me, and I think I am going to faint. Oh no, please, not here, not now! I force myself to stay upright, leaning against the hot wall. I breathe deeply and slowly, then begin to take a few careful steps – I must keep moving.

He is waiting for me, a man wheeling an ancient bike, looking at me with concern. He beckons to me, and I do what I would never normally do – I follow this stranger without any thoughts as to my safety. He takes my rucksack and I yield it without question, my head swimming. Up steps, struggling to get to the top, through a castle and fort, with stunning views which I don't appreciate due to extreme fatigue. Along a narrow street to a building on the corner. He stops, carefully parks his bike at the imposing entrance, then assists me up the steps into a reception area – it's the albergue, thank God. I don't think I can go another inch. I sink onto a bench, while my knight in shining armor speaks to the person dealing with the other pilgrims clamouring for a bed. I don't know what he says, but I am conveyed in a lift straight to the dormitory, no need to queue, my rucksack hung on a stout hook, and given a blanket. When he is satisfied that I am safe, he says gravely, "Buen Camino", then he disappears. A single feather drifts down from nowhere into the space where he stood and brushes my arm, tickling. Later, when I venture downstairs to pay, I find he has already done so. Not just a knight, but an angel.

The dormitory is a long, long hall, with small cell-like rooms on the widow side, each holding four bunkbeds. There is no door on any of them. It's still hot outside, but this a cool, calm, place with shiny wooden floors, white walls, and as boots have to be left on the boot racks provided, people move about quietly. I allow myself to doze but I have a massive headache, so I get off my bed, and wander to the window, to lean my forehead against the cool glass. Listlessly, I gaze out , and I can hardly believe my eyes. This building is on a height, and looks out over the rooftops down to a swimming pool, which is just visible through the gap. I waste no time in throwing things into a plastic bag, and I speed down through the streets, until I finally am standing in eager anticipation at the traffic lights, headache rapidly receding.

There are three pools, a play park, a couple of restaurants and a bar. All open, all free to pilgrims! I sip a cocktail with a cherry on a stick and a tiny paper umbrella, my feet dangling in the silky water. Every bit of me is satisfied.

Later in the evening, I dine outside in the fabulous main Plaza. The atmosphere is lively, the buzz of conversation and laughter rising in the air. The hotel where Hemmingway lived when in Pamplona is just beside me, and the wonderful baroque style café he frequented has a queue going right around the corner. I stroll around the square, stopping frequently to talk or share a memory of the day with other pilgrims. Dining outside in balmy air, with no fear of the tablecloth blowing away, or of sudden downpours, is something that is a novelty to the Irish. In Ireland, if you haven't been there, it is only possible about 'once in a blue moon' ….. if that's not a familiar phrase to you, it means ' almost never!' It's just one of the many things I love about Spain. Carolina, a girl from Barcelona who I had walked with for a while today, waves me over to introduce her fiancé, and we amuse ourselves in counting the number of nationalities we met today. I give up when I reach seventeen, and bid them goodnight, promising to meet tomorrow. I love Pamplona, it's magic.

2 am. This albergue was once the residence of young girls who were training to become nuns, they had almost no possessions, and they had only such clothes as would fit on the hook on the wall near their bed. Each little doorless cubicle held four people. I am afraid to move in case another piece of a broken bed spring digs into my body …… this bed is a torture rack! God help the nuns!

PART FIVE

ON THE WAY TO PUENTE LA REINA.

I am trying to leave Pamplona. The morning is cool, the sky a milky blue, and my rucksack weighs at least one thousand tons. Yes, I am finding it hard to leave Pamplona, mainly because I'm lost. I make a wrong turn at every junction, going further and further away from anywhere recognisable, getting more and more disgruntled by the minute. At last I just sit down on the kerb and sulk. This is not very productive, as there is no-one to care about my frowning visage, but I indulge myself anyway.

After a few minutes, two young men who are sauntering along the street stop and sit down beside me. One has a magnificent Mohican hair do, with multiple piercings, the other is a picture of social decorum with a suit and neat hair, a pair of worn sandals on his feet spoiling the effect somewhat. I am expecting them to ask if I need help, but they smile and without saying anything, begin to sing, softly at first, and gradually I realise that I know this song, so I join in. Some more passers-by add their voices, then along comes Carolina from Barcelona and our impromptu choir gives a rousing modern rendition of 'Amazing Grace' in a mixture of accents and languages. I am now on my feet again, and we embrace each other heartily, then with a smiling 'Buen Camino' we are on our way, Carolina in the lead. I am smiling too, my sulks quite forgotten.

We make our way out of the city, through the pretty village of Cizur Manor, out in the countryside. Stubble fields stretch away on each side of a narrow track, golden in the morning light, and a flock of sheep passes by us. We draw over to the side of the track a little nervously, as three sheep dogs shrink away from us on the other side, equally nervous of strange people as we are of strange dogs. We wander along, not yet into the rhythm of our more brisk walking pace, heat building as the morning draws towards hot noontime. An old man is coming towards us, walking very slowly, leaning on two stout walking sticks, and he stops to chat. My Spanish is not equal to the task, so I wait while he and Carolina converse. Then he speaks to me, shaking the stick to emphasis something – I just smile and nod. But now he is agitated, trying to make some point, and I appeal to Carolina for translation.

"Take the stick," she says, "he wants you to take the stick".

"But he'll fall over without it, look at the way he's leaning on it – he needs it for himself!" I say in alarm.

More animated speech, then Carolina says that he will be deeply offended if I don't take it, so I give up and take it, thanking him, though fearful for his needs. As soon as I have it, he bids us 'Buen Camino' and we part company. I turn to watch his progress, but he seems fine, no need to worry. The stick is quite heavy, with a metal tip, and a woven grip, and actually is quite easy to use. The thought has crossed my mind that I should discard it when I am well out of the old man's sight, but now I feel ashamed of that thought, and vow to keep it as long as it is practical.

The track now rises sharply towards the village of Zariquiegui – see If you can pronounce that! There are more pilgrims on the track, and there's much banter as we walk, quickening our pace a little. We reach the village, to discover a tiny Church with a magnificent Romanesque doorway. People are arriving for Mass, and we remember that It's Sunday, so we follow in behind them. The inside of the church is amazing in the fact that it is without any ornate decoration, apart from one cross on the wall behind a stone slab which is the altar. The sole source of colour comes from the light streaming through narrow stained-glass windows, and there is a palpable air of peace and stillness.

The congregation is small, I counted only eighteen people including children and we are the only pilgrims in the gathering. I try to follow what is being said and catch a little of the meaning of the priest's words, I am sure it is from the gospel of James, always a challenging one. Then the congregation rises and begins to sing. The sound is totally unexpected, pure and beautiful, I have never heard anything so sincere, so sweet, so moving in my life. We are in awe of the sound, and just listen, enthralled. When it is finished, we continue on our way in silence, overcome with gratitude for the privilege of hearing such music. I think of how truculent I was at the start of today, and how uplifted I now am, my heart swelling so my frown is replaced by a silly grin, I just can't stop smiling, the music is still in my head.

Going through the village, the track narrows even more, up, up steeply to the Alto del Perdon, where there is a huge wrought iron pilgrim monument. It didn't look very high from the village, but it is so steep that I bless the old man who gave me the walking stick, it's being put to great use now! Here, the road meets the Camino briefly, and there are pilgrims who are leaving at this point due to other commitments. Many of them will return in the years ahead to this spot and resume their journey. Carolina and her fiancée are going home, and they must stop here. There is a small lay-by with picnic tables and benches, so we have our lunch together before our good bye.

The descent from Alto de Perdon is steep and treacherous underfoot. I slither and slide over sharp scree and large boulders, trying to avoid any damage to the newly planted oak woodland. I breathe heavily, the dust and heat a painful cocktail in my throat. I hear grunts and groans around me, but I see nobody. Somewhere ahead of me, a young man begins to sing in Spanish, and I know the tune so I join in, and other voices in other languages add to the impromptu concert. There is a lightness of spirit in the voices, and I catch laughter bubbling along with each note. Then one of the unseen singers reaches the path that goes all the way to Puente la Reina, and he calls out a joyous

'Buen Camino' and the concert is over. He is gone by the time I reach the path, but I am still singing inside of me.

It seems a long way to Puente la Reina. The path is pleasant, but the heat is just too much – I never thought I'd say that. I have no water left, and I feel sick and dizzy. There are no other people walking, having sensibly stopped, but I, being too hasty, am plodding along in the hottest part of the day. A sign scrawled on a piece of cardboard lies sideways in a laneway, and a roughly drawn arrow points to the left. It says 'Cafe'. Do I pass by, as it might be a very long way off the path, or take a chance on it being near enough to warrant the extra effort? Oh I just can't go any further, so I turn onto the lane, hoping there are no territorial dogs along the way. Soon, the lane leads to a single deserted street, with a glimpse of a bar at the end. There is a small table with an umbrella leaning at a drunken angle, and underneath the table lies a furry heap of sleeping dogs, who don't even open an eye as I sit down. The door into the bar is open, and it looks as if everyone who lives here is crammed into the inadequate space inside, all talking at once. The waiter hurries out, bringing a salad and a bottle of red wine without asking me what I would like, but as there's no menu to be seen, I accept it gratefully. It's delicious.

Fortified by food and drink, I finally stagger into Puente la Reina. I secure the last bed, a lower bunk, thank goodness. The dormitory is light and airy, there is a small reading room, clean showers and a very helpful hospitalero. Outside, there is a fenced off grassy slope leading down to a river, where feet can dangle in the dark water. A donkey is tethered to the fence, but not allowed in. Two long clothes lines and a restaurant nearby complete the picture.

This place is perfect.

I quickly sort out my gear, and hurry out to lie on the cool grass. Somehow, I can't relax. Why do I feel at odds with everything around me? There's an underlying discontent in my mind and I do not feel well disposed towards my fellow pilgrims. I observe those around me with an inward unkind criticism, and then wonder why I have become so sour.

I do not know anyone here, there are no familiar faces at all. Am I jealous because everyone seems to have someone to talk to, except me? I resolve to break this destructive train of thought, and I make a few attempts to engage in conversation, but it peters out. That's when I know what's the matter. I'm lonely! That's something I never normally admit to, but pride is a painful companion and now I just want someone to talk to. Imagine that! This can't be me. But nobody seeks me out, and so I do the only thing I can, I go to my bunk and sleep.

“Wake up! Wake up!”

Hands are shaking me, voices are all around me.

“What? What’s the matter? Is there a fire?” I mumble sleepily, sitting up.

“Get up, come on! We are all going together, but we must hurry, there will be no tables left!”

I flop back on the bed, but then I sit bolt upright. Two words stand out. ‘All’, and ‘Together’

I see my fellow pilgrims urging me to hurry, hopping from one foot to another, but waiting, nevertheless, waiting.

For me.

For a minute, I can’t move with a guilty remembrance of my thoughts earlier, but then I get ready in record time and soon I am sitting outside in the plaza, eating, talking, laughing, all loneliness forgotten. Nearby, there is a cake shop, and I drool over the selection, eventually buying more than I can possibly eat. It is owned by a Portuguese family, and I get to use the only three words I know in Portuguese. I would tell them to you if I could but I’ve forgotten them, but I won’t forget those delicious cakes.

PART SIX

I CAN'T SING.

There seems to be an inordinate amount of singing on this journey, as I look back over these pages. I can't sing. I never sing when at home, yet here, it's as though something has been released in me, and I can't stop it. I pity anyone who has to listen to my singing, as I have a voice that grates horribly on my nerves, never mind anyone else. Also, I am one of those annoying people who remembers all the words of any song I have heard more than twice, so I never run out of songs to sing. I am completely tuneless, I wouldn't even recognise 'Jingle Bells' if you didn't sing the words.

I have a little brown book that fits in the palm of my hand. It was given to me by a man called Joe White, more than twenty years ago, when I was in hospital, recovering from cancer. It's a Gideon Bible, which contains just the New Testament and Psalms, and it has gone with me on every journey I've made since then. I love to read the Psalms, they are written by someone who is just a messed up human being like me, uncertain one minute, praising the next. The writer has all the emotions I have, being angry, querulous, sad, penitent, disbelieving, thankful, and many more. Often, he just cries, asking "Why me?" The words seem to be straight out of my own heart, when there is no other place to run to and no-one else left to call on but God.

Psalm 40.

"I waited patiently for the Lord;

He turned to me and heard my cry.

He lifted me out of the slimy pit,

Out of the mud and mire,

He set my feet on a rock

And gave me a firm place to stand.

He put a new song in my mouth,

A hymn of praise to our God."

PART SEVEN

NEXT STOP, LORCA.

This is a beautiful morning; the sun is coming up and I cross the bridge out of Puente la Reina. I have no particular target to reach, I'll just stop where I want to. The path is a smooth sandy track and I swing along contentedly, singing quietly. Suddenly, without warning, I fall heavily, crashing to the ground, face down. How did this happen? I lie still, checking for damage and –wow! Just four or five inches from my face is a beautiful pale green stick insect! He's so beautiful, I could kiss him! I admire him, he inspects me and we stay there, eyeball to eyeball, until a couple come marching steadily around the bend. They halt, then rush forward in alarm, seizing me and attempting to haul me up, while I protest vigorously. There's only one of me and two of them, and I fail utterly to explain that I wish to commune with a stick insect a little longer as they set me up on my feet. They only speak what I think is a Scandinavian language, so they are mystified when I begin searching the ditch all around for something obviously precious. They begin to look around too, probably thinking I have dropped my purse or something, so I call a halt to this crazy safari, thanking them for their concern. When they are satisfied that I am not about to expire, they continue on their way. I whisper a goodbye in the general direction of where I met the stick insect and walk away, elated by the encounter. I'm sure they think I'm mad.

Today, the landscape I pass through is rural, skirting vineyards, olive trees, fruit trees and small fields of vegetables of every kind, huge yellow pumpkins lolling on the warm earth. The sky goes on forever and on a hill in the distance is the tiny village of Cirauqui, looking like a squashed straw hat on the top. The rhythm of walking brings all my senses into harmony, and I don't want it to end. What a privilege to be free, to have choices in my life. I am acutely aware that so many women throughout the world do not have the freedom I enjoy. Time to be thankful!

The very small Plaza Mayor in Cirauqui is entered through a roman archway, and about four strides away is the exit through another impressive arch, also dating from roman times. There is a tobacconist's shop on one side, and a small grocery store on the opposite side, and that is as far as commerce goes in Cirauqui. The locals congregate at the tobacconist shop, the pilgrims take one of the few metal chairs outside the grocery store. It becomes evident that locals always know best, as this Plaza is on a significant slope, and it is necessary to sit sideways, feet firmly planted, an uncomfortable strain on the knees, if you don't wish to slide with a metallic scrape into the lap of the tobacconist and his customers.

To the pilgrim, chairs on the pavement mean 'cafe', but not to the proprietor of this shop. He sells groceries, and if you want tea or coffee, there's a hit and miss machine on the wall. If you want sandwiches, he will not sell single tomatoes, or half baguettes, you must buy the ingredients as he sees fit, half a kilo of tomatoes, a huge baguette, a half block of butter and five or six thick slices of ham. He never answers questions, no matter what language is used. Under the second arch, there is a niche which holds the sello, and so I stamp my pilgrim passport with what is very thick, purple ink, it oozes out from between the pages and stains everything it touches. Up through little narrow, winding streets, around a corner, and I am once again happily alone.

In this golden land, the sun makes nonsense of pastel shades, instead colouring the sky hard, bright cobalt blue, the stubble fields rich cadmium yellow. The olive trees, lovingly and skilfully tended, sit neatly in patterns that fit into the curves of the land, the vines stand in straight rows, and the ploughed earth is a deep ochre. Underfoot is a cobbled roman road – strange to think of those long ago who walked the same path as I now walk, with the same hopes, prayers and dreams.

And so to Lorca. Over a roman bridge – what else? And up the last steep, short rise in to the village. The first building on the right is a huge church, Romanesque of course, and on the left a row of small houses. Three grannies are passing a little child between them, and they call to me to admire the baby, a girl called Rosita, about five months old. I get to cuddle her, while the grannies show me the things they each have made for her pram, lacy pillow cases, crochet blankets and more, all spotlessly white. I don't know which are her real grannies, but they seem happy to share the joy. They tell me that the sello is in the church, which is locked, but I snoop around the building and find it on a window sill, ink almost dried out, but it makes enough of a mark to satisfy me.

Lorca has few inhabitants, and is either charming to the traveller or just somewhere to pass through. There is absolutely nothing to do in Lorca. For me, it is charming and I resolve to stay there tonight. I wander along the short street which winds in and out haphazardly, and come to the only bar I can see. There's nobody about, so I leave my rucksack behind the bar, and walk back the couple of hundred yards to a fountain, with two long benches either side. The walls of every home are bright white, with red geraniums in window boxes, or attached to the walls, the red blooms vivid against the white. I soak up the sun, dozing peacefully with the tinkling music of the fountain lulling me to sleep. Not a soul is stirring. My head drops and I wake with a start. The heat is fierce and unrelenting, and I walk down again to the bar, which is almost the last house in the village. There is no albergue in Lorca, but a small pension is attached to the bar, and I manage to catch up with the eager young man who runs it with his grandmother. Clean and as spotless as it can be, it is also cheap, and it is with some relief that I lie down for a siesta.

Later, I sit in the bar, so far the only customer. The young man offers me a glass of his grandmother's lemonade, and it's absolutely wonderful. I have another, sipping slowly to prolong the pleasure. He is keen to improve his

English and I am keen to improve my Spanish, so we chat about life in our different countries, our hopes and dreams, and food. He is very proud of his grandmother's cooking and I hope for his sake that more people come to enjoy it.

Dinner is served at eight, and by then a polite young man from Korea, two giggling young French girls, an earnest lady from Belgium and a German couple have checked in. We sit at the only table, an international family, as the first course arrives. There is no menu, we take what comes, and it is a pasta dish with an amazing sauce, followed by a stew full of flavour and tender meat, then an apple pie of enormous proportions, served with a large jug of fragrant custard. The grandmother does not appear at any time, though we would love to compliment her on her skill in the kitchen.

After dinner discussions are always interesting, and we quiz the young Korean, who is most informative. Everyone joins in on many topics, but the lady from Belgium says nothing at all, to anyone about anything, she remains completely silent all through dinner and after. Then, without warning, she rises and subjects us to a five-minute diatribe on the evils of flippancy and laughter, we are not serious, apparently. She sweeps out of the room, and the French girls let a small giggle escape, and soon we are all laughing helplessly.

It was a lovely day, and a happy evening. From my bedroom window, I look out over the red tiled rooftops, moonlight casting deep shadows. I think about my moodiness in Puente la Reina, wondering why I felt so lonely there, amongst such a crowd, yet here, where there is nothing and nobody except the few diners, I feel really happy and content. I turn out the light and lie still as moonlight pours into the room and drift off, dreamless.

In the morning, the young man presents me with a huge wedge of apple pie, wrapped up well, for my journey. He stands at the door until I am out of sight, waving.

PART EIGHT

FREE GRATIS.

Ruby red liquid splashes over my hands as I clumsily fill a narrow-necked water bottle. This can't be real! I lick the back of my hand and mmm, it's real, alright. A tap in the wall of this bodega, that wine, not water, flows from. A queue forms behind me, but I take my time, fiddling with the lid, careful to screw it on tight – I don't want to lose any of it. I turn away, and collide with one of the Italians that I last saw in Roncesavalles. He gathers me in a huge hug, and gestures towards the fountain, a wide smile on his face.

He breaks into rapid Italian, I only recognize a few words, but it is clear that the local population have been trying to speed them on their way, as they have been here for three days. Their belongings lie abandoned at the roadside and they slumber blissfully in the morning sun. They remind me of another comfortable heap beneath a table a few days ago, sleeping untroubled by haste or necessity, but the one young man awake is keen to move on now, so we start to throw water over his friends, and gradually they stir, and finally rise.

I leave them to it, trying to decide if it would be wise to empty my other water bottle, and fill it with wine instead. I think to myself that this will probably never happen to me again in my life, so I sensibly opt for – the wine.

It's a long, dusty way to the next village, and I dawdle along under the hot sun, revelling in the beauty of the landscape. I peer into the vegetation along the path, which is alive with tiny miracles - flowers, insects, geckos and butterflies that I have only seen in books – purple hairstreaks, white admirals, and something blue I don't recognize. I hear the footsteps of people coming up behind me, and it's two of the Italian young men, who have easily caught me at my slow pace. We chat to one another, laughing all the time, as we have no common language and have no idea what we're saying to each other. Sometimes it's nice just to be really silly.

We spot something on the path in front of us, and, careful not to step on it, we halt to take some photos. It's a beautiful moth, it's wings spread out, showing a fascinating, intricate design, like a gown of black and gold. I've never seen anything like it, and I have not ever been able to identify it since. If I hadn't got my few grainy photos, I would think I imagined it.

Now the track runs through fields of stubble, with enormous bales of hay stacked like skyscrapers here and there. It's time for lunch. Sheltering from the constant glare of the sun, we sit in the shade of the stack of bales nearest to us, spreading out our food on a couple of plastic bags, sharing everything. We are joined by a few more and it's so dreamy, eating, drinking free wine, sharing, lying back and allowing myself to drift off, peaceful silence. I could stay like this forever.

I don't remember who heard it first, but there's a low rumble in the distance, and we begin to sit up, one by one. Is it thunder? It's getting louder and louder, nearer and nearer. Suddenly a massive, giant-sized tractor with menacing metal prongs sweeps towards us out of nowhere, showing no sign of slowing. We scramble frantically out of the way, as he stabs the bales, a modern dinosaur with long sabre-like teeth. Our lunch goes flying everywhere, wine spilling into the dry earth like blood, the tractor roaring away in a shower of fumes and dust, leaving us a little shocked. I wonder could he have stopped if one of us had stumbled or fallen. The others are lamenting the loss of the wine, but never mind.

I draw carefully from my rucksack….my second water bottle. Cheers!

Later, in the quiet period between siesta and dinner, I lie on my bunk, turning over in my mind all that I saw today. I come to the conclusion that no matter what theories I have heard of the Big Bang, Black Holes etcetera, there must be a Creator, none of this can be a chance happening, a random coming together of particles. Call it what you will. I am content to call it God.

High noon in Los Arcos.

It's noon when I walk into Los Arcos. The air is full of yellow dust that scrapes the back of my throat with every breath. Nothing stirs, it's as if the population have vanished, and the town is like the Marie Celeste – eerily silent. There seems to be an excessive amount of cow dung in the street, and I pick my way carefully on the baked earth. A torn poster catches my eye, and then I understand. There has been a bullfight, or there's going to be one, and the stout planks wedged against doorways and alleyways are there to keep the bulls moving on by. No chance of a bull in the china shop, then.

The deserted dusty street, the silent suspense, remind me of some cowboy film, and I feel that I am not dressed for the part. I should at least have a gun and holster, and a wide brimmed hat. Meandering along, I pass through the Plaza Mayor, and at last hear the sound of voices. I turn a corner and a wall of noise envelopes me. A café bar, absolutely jam packed with what seems to be every man, woman and child from the town. They besiege the bar, ten deep, pushing, leaning on one another, while those who have managed to get served are trying to wriggle through the press of bodies back to their seats, coffee spilling everywhere.

It transpires that the annual fiesta, including bull fighting, was yesterday, and the citizens are suffering from one gigantic, communal hangover. Even the barmen, who wince each time the coffee machine screeches and steams.

I sit down for a while, but I don't attempt to get a drink, it's far too busy, and their need is greater than mine! There's a slight air of lawlessness in this place, and as I leave, I expect a posse in pursuit of a bank robber at least, to gallop past.

PART NINE

MEDIEVAL VIANA.

I am beginning to think that I have inadvertently taken a ride in a time machine, as I approach Viana, yet another exquisite medieval town. The approach to the town is a long straight yellow ochre stretch of sandy earth, which leads slightly uphill to merge with the colour of the walls and houses. I am walking in a dream, hundreds of years back. A man on a horse canters leisurely by, little puffs of dust rising as hooves hit the dry ground. A sturdy senora of mature years is coming towards me, rosary beads in her hands, dressed in black. She stops to talk. We are both proud of our small amount of each other's language, and she enquires about my journey so far. When she was young, she tells me, she walked to Leon, but had no time to go any further. Now she thinks it's too late, but when we discover that we are the same age, she smiles and says 'maybe'

A car comes past, and I am almost shocked by its presence in this medieval moment. A languid hand waves from the passenger side, and the car fades away, becoming a carriage drawn by two white horses, the lady dressed in a pale silvery gown, Her hand as she waves, is heavy with rings studded with precious stones….where was I? Oh yes, the senora and I wish each other 'Buen Camino', and I reach the outskirts of the town. I sit down on a bench, intending to rest for a moment before looking for an albergue, but a loud bang makes me leap to my feet. What was that? And being from Northern Ireland, I immediately assume that it's someone shooting. I see people running up a side street, so I follow them. They are not running in fear but to catch a glimpse of the bulls which are about to run around the streets, corralled by wooden barriers. I have stumbled on another fiesta. The bulls run every few hours, and the young men of the town, and some not so young, run ahead of the bulls until they have nearly been caught, then they vault over the barriers to safety. This is supposed to show how brave the men are, but by the time the bulls are running for the last time, they are not a bit interested, they just trot around like dozy cows.

'Never mind the bulls, Pauline, get somewhere to sleep.' I am so tired and dirty that a shower sounds like heaven, so off I go to the albergue to check in. A nun sits at a desk facing the door, so she can see who is pushy or not, and we, the pilgrims, are treated like naughty children. Her face is incapable of smiling, and she confiscates all our boots as one by one we sign in. Luckily, I have sandals for wearing when I'm not walking, but some are not so lucky, and bare feet are suddenly fashionable. We are told sternly not to go to the fiesta, we are pilgrims, not tourists. She will be locking the door at precisely ten o'clock. Some of us make the mistake of trying to soften her a little, begging for even half an hour extra time, but it falls on very deaf ears. Instead she shoots such a venomous look our way that we scramble to get out of the room and off to our allocated dormitory. We have been handed a numbered ticket, which is the number of our bed, so as there are three large rooms, we have a few giggles trying to find the one we are to sleep in.

Oh, shock horror! For the first time in my life I am confronted with triple bunks, and there's no way I can manage that. Not only are they so high, but the space in between where we are expected to sleep is just about wide enough to get into – a bit like trying to slip into an envelope. The dormitory I am in has sixteen Frenchmen who are cycling the Camino, two more Irish ladies and myself. And one empty bunk, which goes across the bottom of mine. Every possible inch of space is used, but somehow, one of the French cyclists who can't bear to be separated from his wheels has managed to smuggle his bike into the dorm. He covers the spare bunk with some plastic and then tenderly lays the bike on it. I fully expect him to kiss it goodbye before he goes off to the showers.

Well, I don't want to waste a minute for exploring this enchanting town, so after a quick shower I hasten out into the sunshine, scuttling past the scowling boot stealer, free. To make things even better, one of the French cyclists has kindly swopped tickets with me so I have a middle bunk. I stroll along, thinking about getting some food. Siesta is taken very seriously in northern Spain, everywhere closes at two o'clock, so I sit down in the sun at the first café I come to, as it's just half-past one. Soon, I tuck into an omelette, accompanied by a salad of mammoth proportions, and clutched in my fist, a glass of chilled vino blanco.

As I enjoy my lunch, I ponder on the difference between the nun at Roncesavalles and the nun in the albergue here. A thought occurs to me. The nun here is very disapproving of fiesta, fun and late hours. So why does she shut up sixteen Frenchmen and three Irish ladies in a room for the night?

Stalls in the market had been selling fabulous fresh vegetables and fruit, brightly coloured clothes, aromatic spices, sizzling paella, bric-a-brac of every description, cured meats, and much more. But the stallholders have disappeared for their siesta, and just two small boys of about ten years old are hanging about, watching to see if anyone wishes to make a purchase. I would love to buy some of the produce, but I have no desire to spend time in the tiny kitchen at the albergue while the sun is shining outside, and as for the clothes, well, sadly there is no room in my rucksack for unnecessary purchases.

There is plenty of time to explore, and I wander through narrow streets, unchanged for nearly a thousand years, the cobbles underfoot worn smooth with the passage of generations. In and out of churches, drowsily sitting a while in small plazas with vibrant gardens, beside sparkling, chuckling fountains. It is easy to slip into a reverie, imagining that I am again transported back in time. Now I am an old duenna, who is neglecting her duties of chaperone to the daughter of a stern Duke. I am watching and waiting, anxious, until at last she comes from the cool dark of a nearby house, laughing as she turns to blow kisses at someone unseen, blushing prettily, her skirts flowing around her neat ankles as she steps towards me. She scolds me gently for my anxiety, saying surely I should have trusted her to come back quickly.

A hand laid on my shoulder startles me into wakefulness. No, it is not an irate noble parent, it is an elderly lady admonishing me for falling asleep under the full glare of the hot sun. She invites me to come with her, so arm in arm we walk slowly to her house, which is a collection of ground floor rooms underneath her son's home. It is charmingly cluttered with her belongings, and I am seated on a wide armchair, plied with coffee and tiny sweet biscuits. We communicate sporadically, when either one of us manages to stammer out a few hesitant sentences in our two languages. She says it is a blessing to look after peregrinos, it is a pleasure for her to get this chance. I spend the rest of the afternoon here with my new friend, and later we cook a meal together. Her name is Loli, and we decide to go to the evening fiesta together, where there will be music, parades, and of course, the running of the bulls.

The town is packed, bands are assembling in some distant street, and nearby, children are giving a demonstration of a country dance. The bands arrive, marching into the magnificent colonnaded Plaza Mayor. They take their seats around the square, taking turns to provide music to which a few brave souls are dancing. Loli enthusiastically joins in, but I have a deep-seated horror of dancing in public, so I watch, enjoying her enjoyment. Soon there is a crowd of whirling, swirling couples dancing energetically, as more and more take to the wooden platform laid out for them. A little gnome of a man, with roguish eyes, and at least eighty years on this earth, crosses the square to ask a young girl to dance. She is obviously a pilgrim, wearing boots and shorts, but she gamely gets to her feet and waltzes around, her partner holding her a little too close for comfort. His grasp gets tighter, and the girl looks a trifle alarmed - but relief is at hand. A little lady, even smaller than the little man, marches through the dancers, her back ramrod straight, her eyes full of anger. She walks up to the couple, and taps the man on the shoulder. He turns around, and before his face can register his surprise, she draws back her arm and smacks him soundly on the cheek. Her friends commend her with a cheer, as she then grasps him firmly and painfully by the ear to lead him home.

Like a real Cinderella, I must be back in the albergue by ten o'clock, so Loli and I say a tearful goodbye, with promises to meet again in the future. It is hard to part, and I pass the doorkeeper's scowls without a glance.

There's someone in my bunk.

It's a female, with a long plait of blonde hair hanging over the side of the bunk. She's awake, and stares at me as though I am the intruder.

"I'm sorry, but I think you have the wrong bunk," I say, not very convincingly.

"But no, I must sleep here" she replies in a French accent. "The snoring man from Sweden is in the other room, and I need to sleep."

She turns away from me, as though that is the end of the matter, pulling her sleeping bag up around her ears. Suddenly, I get angry, and cease to be polite. I am tired and I want my bunk!

"Get out of my bunk, please. Now."

She ignores me, so I say very loudly, "Get out of my bunk please!"

"There is another – you can use that one," she says, over her shoulder. "I like this one."

It really doesn't matter which bunk I sleep in but she has piled her belongings on the spare one, and dumped mine on the floor, so I think she should at least pick them up. Most of the cyclists are in their sleeping bags, wide awake and watching the altercation. One of them, the one who swapped beds with me earlier, sits up and speaks to her. They argue for a moment or two, then sulkily she heaves herself out of the bunk, gathers her belongings and moves to the spare bunk. She falls asleep before I am tucked up myself, and all is calm for a few minutes. Then she begins to snore, deep rolling exhalations, and in minutes, we are all awake, except the Irish ladies who seem to be stone deaf. All through the long night, it goes on, despite our attempts to stop her. The cyclists throw things at her, they shake her and pinch her, roll her over, but she is absolutely sound asleep. Around five o'clock, when it's too late to hope for any respite anyway, she wakes up. In a matter of minutes, she is packed and ready to leave, and she disappears out into the dark, refreshed and off to an early start.

Groggy and exhausted, the rest of us have just one hour to doze a bit, before another day begins. I wonder what the 'snoring man' she mentioned was like, he must have been spectacular on the snorer's scale! As I take the narrow laneway out of wonderful Viana, I wonder where the bicycle that was nestled on the spare bunk went. Is it tucked up with its loving owner or out with the others, but I suppose I'll never know now.

PART TEN

JUST TRUDGING ALONG.

Have I been walking too fast? Not drinking enough water? Whatever is the case, my legs feel so heavy that it's as though they are filled with cement, my spirits are so low, and I think I would like to go home now. Perhaps a pilgrim is meant to be lonely or homesick, then we will call on Him even more. Or maybe God only wants me to help someone else as I journey on, and it, the camino that is, is not really for me at all. Will I recognize that person, that opportunity? I trudge along, passing through villages without noticing, the black dog trailing behind, and all the while that irritating tremor in my left hand is really persistent. It carries a warning for me that I try to ignore. Yes, maybe I should go home.

"Buen Camino!"

A cheery group of young Australians pass me and I force myself to reply, hoping they will keep on going, I don't want to talk, I haven't the energy. They walk on by, and I am sad that I can't seem to respond to anyone today. The path here meets a collection of concrete circles with a bewildering number of road signs – I follow the familiar yellow arrows into a dark underpass. It is dank and smells awful, and what looks like a heap of old clothes is actually several people sleeping on the wet, stinking concrete. As I pass by, one of them staggers to his feet, calling 'Miguel! Miguel!' He is waving a syringe, and he lurches towards me,

'Miguel! Miguel!' his voice echoes off the walls.

But I am so numb that I just walk on past him, not even capable of fear. I feel cold, even though the sun is shining, and I am relieved to see in the distance the next town, Santo Domingo de Calazada. When I finally check into the nearest albergue, I only want to sleep. It is early afternoon and pilgrims are moving around the light, airy open plan dormitories, sun streaming in from every window. Another fiesta is gearing up for a parade outside, and there is plenty of laughter and noise. I take about three seconds to fall soundly asleep, crashing onto the bed face down, legs hanging over the side, abandoning my rucksack to where it fell.

Hours later, I wake up. It's dark outside. There's nobody in the room except myself, and just below the window an ear-splitting band is playing as badly as anything I've ever heard. I am arranged neatly on the bed, someone must have tucked me securely in. A head pokes around the door and I see it is the man who checked the pilgrims in earlier. He smiles and asks if I am alright, telling me that I have slept for almost seven hours. Then he disappears for a few minutes, returning with tea and toast for me. He is concerned that I might be ill, but I assure him that I was only tired, so tired, and now I am rested. He chats for a few minutes, and tells me that there is enough hot water for a shower – and as there is a fiesta, there is no curfew. So just a short time later, I walk out into the crowds thronging the streets. I eat food from some of the stalls, sampling little pieces of tapas, and a long cool beer with lemonade in it. I am at last starting to relax, though tiredness still pervades my body, so I slowly make my way back to the albergue. Many of the pilgrims have the same idea, and we sit around, talking about our experiences so far, our different reasons for walking the camino, the people we have met, and I get a chance to thank the man who tucked me in earlier. There are no bunks here, just beds arranged in little alcoves of four, and it is a luxury to be able to sit upright, instead of being crammed in the narrow space between bunks.

The sound of a deep baritone voice rolls out from under the door to the shower room, and everyone waits for the singer to appear, imagining a stout, dark haired Italian, perhaps, mature and assured. A thin fair-haired youth eventually creeps apologetically out, and scuttles to his bed, and when it is established beyond doubt that he is indeed the singer, gets a round of applause. He is prevailed upon to sing some more, and I go to sleep listening to wonderful music in one ear, and a long-winded monologue in the other from the bed beside me, as the occupant, a tall, elderly scholar tries to teach me some words in Latin. I have no idea why.

It's Sunday. I wake up early, just before 5 a.m. The same man who made toast for me yesterday is quietly cleaning the floor, but when he sees me sit up, he signals to me to stay where I am. I think it's because he is loath to waken anyone else, but no, it's because he has made breakfast for me, which he brings to me on a tray. Breakfast in bed! It's so thoughtful, I could cry. He enquires about my health, and advises that I only walk a short distance today. I then find out that he is a doctor, semi-retired, who spends time each year in helping at this albergue, which was at one time his childhood home.

Taking his advice, I make a slow start to the day. I lie in my warm sleeping bag, dozing, as all around me pilgrims get ready for another day's walking. Around eight o'clock, I venture out, having said my goodbyes to the kind doctor, and I wander through the streets, until I come upon a church where Mass is being said. On impulse, I enter, joining those standing at the back, as it looks as though it is full. I am unable to understand much of what is being said by the priest, a small man with a powerful voice, but it is clear that he is unhappy about something. His voice thunders out, his arms wave and he punches the air to emphasis his point. I realize there is no point in staying as I have no idea what's going on, so I turn to leave, bumping into a thin, disheveled woman who had the same idea. I apologise, and she follows me out.

She walks close behind me, almost stepping on my heels, and it's a bit unnerving. I turn off the street into a café, and she follows me in, sitting opposite me, looking expectant. After a few attempts at communication, I understand she is hungry, so I buy us both some food. She gobbles it up in record time, and then reaches across the table to lift my plate, and polishes off that, too. Somehow, I manage to understand her, and so she tells me her story. I am not sure what is fact and what is fiction, so I recount it just as she told me.

She is Austrian, aged fifty-two, and had been walking the camino, until she had arrived at a monastery near Santo Domingo three months ago. The monks offer food and shelter to pilgrims, and she decided to stay that night. Pilgrims were expected to attend evening prayers, and also help clean the accommodation next morning before resuming their walk. She was most enthusiastic, and persuaded the monks to let her stay a second night. Then she asked for a third night, but the monks were a little weary of her intrusive behaviour, and declined. This is the point where I realize she is not quite stable, as she tells me that the reason they won't let her stay is because one of the monks has fallen violently in love with her, and she with him. The other monks are jealous, and want to keep them apart. She had bombarded them with gifts to be given to the hapless monk who had caught her eye, and when the gifts were not accepted, she broke into the monastery, twice. Next, she held a vigil at the gate, so the object of her affection could not leave the safety of the monastery, due to the rather overtly physical nature of those affections which she wishes to bestow on him. Finally, a restraining order was issued against her, and she found herself in custody several times.

Now she has no money left. She is vague as to where she staying, and I suspect that she is sleeping rough. She is filthy and smelly, her skin covered in scrofulous scabs, her grey hair greasy, with bald patches where she has scratched it. She is alarmingly thin. I get up to go to the toilet, and she says she will look after my bag. After a very quick visit, I come back to find her rummaging through my belonging's, completely unabashed. She says she is looking for 'something useful', and I have to pull my bag out of her hands quite forcefully. I never leave anything of value in my rucksack, so it doesn't matter. I put some money on the table for her, and snatching it up, she dashes out the door without looking back. I heave a sigh of relief, waiting a couple of minutes to make sure she has gone. I feel a bit guilty, wondering if there is anything more I should have done, but the thought of that hair erases any desire to seek her out. It's beginning to get hot, so I start walking. After a couple of kilometers, I realize something.

I am singing quietly as I walk, and the black dog is nowhere to be seen.

Black Dog.

He glides along walls,
lurks around corners,
a furtive shadow
disappearing into crevices
seeping through the pavement beneath my feet,
following me relentlessly.
I try to lose him
down the dark alleyways of my mind
but his presence ripples around me,
above me, about me.
His shadow falls on me
like a mourning cloak.

PART ELEVEN

SARDINES.

Walking along in a day-dream, not thinking about anything in particular, just savoring the moment. Not singing, not praying, not talking, just being. Perfect peace. There's nobody else in sight, though there must be some pilgrims at least, in the vicinity. I come to a crossroads, where a few houses cluster together, leaning in like old women gossiping. There's one kiosk which serves as a bar with one chair beside it and an old farmhouse with an optimistic sign above the door. 'Albergue'.

It's cool and dim inside. There is a long sitting room which becomes a dining room and then a kitchen – a convivial open plan arrangement which allows several conversations at once. Surprisingly, it is nearly full and I am glad to secure a bed. Well, not an actual bed, just floor space in the loft, where everyone sleeps in rows, squashed like sardines. Already the floor in one half of the room is full, sleeping bags in rows like body bags, and I add mine, wondering how I will find it later amongst all the others. I have met quite a few of the pilgrims already who have stopped here, and we gather around the long table, enjoying our time together. One of the two monks who run this place tells us we are to have a communal meal at 8 o'clock, and asks would anybody like to help. Soon we are in deep discussion about menus, nutrition, calories and fibre, to name but a few. The kitchen is a hive of activity. My hand is shaking very visibly, but I lift a knife and start chopping vegetables, oblivious to the looks of alarm on those near me. Swiftly, the knife is gently confiscated and replaced by a pen and piece of paper. I am assigned an easier option, giving thanks for the food before we eat. Yet it's not so simple, as there are so many languages amongst us that I'm sure to miss one, if not more.

Outside, the kiosk is closed, but some beer is left on the chair with a note saying 'gratis'. It looks as though the beer might be a trifle warm, so I opt for a drink of tea made by one of the monks, and spend some time praying in a little attic room set aside for that purpose. A man joins me, and as he prays, tears stream down his face, and his body shakes with emotion.

As we begin to assemble for our evening meal, there are new friendships being made, and reunions with pilgrims we have met previously. I find myself enjoying the company of four young Australians, three girls and a young man. They have never been away from Australia before, and they are making the most of this trip. I listen to their enthusiastic young voices as they tell me stories of the adventures they have had. I am struck by their openness to everyone they meet, and their desire to find something to take from the camino, to go with them into their future life.

For a while after dinner, most of the pilgrims gather in the kitchen area, some spilling out on the small patch of grass. The hum of conversation, sudden bursts of laughter, chairs creaking making a pleasant background noise.

I decide to retire for the night, and set off to the loft to try to find my sleeping bag. I am glad I didn't leave it any longer, as it takes a while to locate. I find that the Australians are next to me, the young man being nearest. The room is partially divided by an archway, with a window each end, through which an icy wind is blowing. There is nobody in the last space left in the room, the one beside me. There have been a few stories told about a Swedish man who apparently is the champion of all snorers, and we are giggling about this, when a rucksack is flung down on my other side, a body follows, snuggles into his sleeping bag, and instantly begins to snore. It happens so quickly that it takes a minute or two to realize that this is the champion of all snorers, and we try to stifle our laughter as the sound echoes around the room, and muttered protests are heard, to no avail.

The girls fall asleep, but the young man and I talk quietly into the night. We have much in common, and it is the most interesting and meaningful communication I have had with anyone since beginning the camino. We talk about our different experiences and what impression they have had, and how we react to them.

He tells me that he is gay. Sadly, his mother, who was his constant support and inspiration, died just two years ago of cancer. He has not seen his father since he was eleven. He says he misses his mother, but that she gave him the gift of joy. I am so amazed at his strength of character, and I think she must have been a remarkable woman.

The lights have been turned out but cold moonlight streams in the window, and someone gets up to close the window, stumbling over the bodies packed together on the floor. But a Dutch man sits up, to beg that the window remain open. He shines a torch on the man next to him, and we can see why. It is his brother, who took off his shirt while walking, and has been really badly sunburned, his skin a livid red, and unbearably painful. He is lying beneath the open window to try to cool his burning skin, so of course the window remains open.

There is much rustling and flashes of torchlight as people try to find more clothes to put on. Beside me, my young friend delves among his possessions, finally gleefully showing me his secret weapon – ear plugs, and he is soon sleeping soundly. I have my own secret weapon –diazepam - which I use to overcome my fear of flying. At this point, it is more important to get a good night's sleep than to worry about flying. I put on all the clothes I can fit into, and sleep warmly all night long.

"Pauline! Pauline!"

A gentle hand is trying to shake me awake, an urgent whisper reaching through the fog of sleep. I take a few seconds to remember where I am, then I see it is my young Australian friend.

“Yes, I’m awake. What’s the matter?”

“I need to ask you something” he says.

“Okay, I’m listening”.

“Can I have your address, just in case?”

“Yes, of course, but in case of what?” I ask.

“In case some time, I might need a mother” he whispers.

PART TWELVE

BURGOS IS NOT MY FAVOURITE CITY.

The approach into Burgos seems to be a choice between walking along the edge of a busy motorway, or a short cut through an abandoned industrial dump. I am sure there is a better way somewhere, but I am totally lost, having no idea how to find the correct path. Several others have also found themselves at this point, so after some discussion, we decide to take the short cut. All seems good, and we march confidently into a maze of crates, cardboard, rolls of wire and anything that 'might come in useful someday'. A low growl on my right makes me jump nervously, and we see that guard dogs, mainly Alsatians, are tethered all along the narrow path between each heap. It's too late to retreat, so we weave back and forth, just managing to keep out of reach of their bared fangs, completely unnerved.

Eventually, we reach the center of the city. I decide to go into the Cathedral to calm down and also to pray. However, a doorman stops me in my tracks, saying I must pay to enter. By this time, I am hot, tired and cantankerous, so I loftily inform him that I have no intention of paying to pray, that I consider it a travesty, a blight upon Christianity, etc. etc. Of course, the doorman doesn't understand a word of my long-winded protest, and cares even less. He looks past me, repeating in a completely disinterested tone that I must pay – like everybody else. I give up.

The university in Burgos gives a free meal every day to a limited number of pilgrims, so I wander along the path which follows the river Arlazon, trying not to think how silly I was to make such a fuss at the Cathedral. The canteen at the University is still open, the pilgrim menu is fish, or fish or fish…oh I think I'll have……..fish.

I had hoped to walk on to the next village, but I feel a little bit queasy, so I check into the albergue, which is just beside the University. For the first time on the camino, I am bored. The dormitory has an oppressively low ceiling, and the windows are small, so it's stuffy and headache-inducing. There is nothing in the immediate vicinity of interest, and anyway, I feel too lethargic to explore.

Each pilgrim is given a free ticket to tour the city on a tourist bus when they check in, so I board the bus at 6pm. and off it goes. By 7pm., the bus is parked at the highest point from which to view the city, but only a handful of passengers are enjoying the panorama. Everyone else, including myself, are being violently sick into the bushes. The tour guide is appalled, he is not going to let his nice clean bus be a receptacle for our noxious offerings, so he chivvies those who are not sullying the greenery back onto the bus, and it roars away, leaving us to whatever fate awaits. Gradually, the sickness stops, and we all sit on the kerb, our legs too shaky to hold us up. We try to find what the cause of the great purge is, and conclude it must be the fish in the university canteen. It's the only thing we have all eaten.

Eventually, all the pilgrims are tucked up safely in their sleeping bags, and the lights go out. The peace is short-lived, as a whoosh of foul-smelling water washes out from under the door of the toilet block. Something has gone badly wrong, and as I am in a bunk just beside the toilets, I am obliged to help clean the floor. Oh yuck!

This happens twice more during the night, and in the early morning, I have had enough. By five thirty, I am packed and ready to leave. It's barely light, but I march away, breathing in great gulps of fresh air.

There's no such thing as a free lunch.

Scorched Earth

I love this land,
This scorched place, my chosen mother earth.
I love this red soil,
Red, red.
Fields of sunflowers,
Poppies amongst the corn –
The furnace-heat of noontime,
Hot smell of ploughed earth after sundown.
Hot colours – yellow, red, blood-red
Ochre, raw umber, burnt sienna –
I love this place.
For this,
I left the cold embrace of my birth land.

Wet with her constant tears,
I never saw her beauty.
Bone-chilled in soul and heart,
I could not rejoice in green hills
Smudged by wisping mists,
Nor feeble light that could never overcome
The bulging threat of her grey skies
Grey, grey-blue, grey-black.
Sad drooping flowers in Spring
Smells of damp earth everywhere.
The smell of everything damp
Damp.

Oh, I remember
Everything

Damp.

I will never leave this place,
This blue sky,
This yellow sky.
Some day, my dust will mingle
With this dust
And I will be complete.

But sometimes,
I dream about rain.

PART THIRTEEN

MESETA, WHERE DREAMS AWAIT

I am having an early breakfast, sitting contentedly in the square of a small village. Feeling a little smug, as for once I seem to be ahead of most other pilgrims who were in the albergue last night. I pay for my food, scraping the metal chair on the pavement as I stand up, the sound setting my teeth on edge. Checking for the yellow arrows, I walk away, head down, thinking of this and that, almost sleepwalking. Before I know it, I am in the small settlement of Rabe de Las Calzadas. It's going to be a hot, hot day and I would like to buy some extra water.

Nothing stirs, there seems to be no movement behind the shutters on every window, and it's impossible to find which one is a shop, or if there is a shop at all. I dither about a bit, reluctant to walk any further without extra water. A light tap on my shoulder startles me and when I turn round, a tiny, very elderly nun in a grey habit is standing there. She holds out a piece of ribbon with a medal on it, smiling a little nervously. I take it, twisting around to put it in the elastic pocket on my rucksack. When I turn back, she has gone. How odd.

Eager to move on, I pass by the silent houses, until I am back on the dusty track, leaving Rabe sleeping. The meseta starts here, a high, cold tableland where oats, barley and wheat are grown, sometimes interspersed with fields of sunflowers. I have been walking with my head down, watching my feet over the rough ground. Now the land falls away as the high point is gained, and I lift my head.

My diary for that day says simply:

"Brilliant! Brilliant meseta! I love it! I love it! Wow, full sun! hot, hot! I love it!"

I can't convey how I seem to explode into space and light, all the particles of me merging with the endless sky, the vast earth. I have no words to express how everything wonderful I ever imagined is spread before me, - light, colour, sound, silence, smells, space, stillness. It's as though God has cast all this from His hand, like a sower scattering seed, saying,

"See, this is what I can do, this is what I have given you."

Meseta, where my dreams live. What is it that makes me feel this way? Is it the light, the depth of colour, the unseen pulsing life of all the tiny things I love? Or the sky that forms a high cathedral over me, disappearing into heaven, far above? The sense of coming home? I stumble as I slowly turn in a complete circle, arms outstretched, head tilted back. A little wave of dizziness makes me lose my balance and I sit down heavily on the ground, laughing. I lie back and drink in the sky above me, letting it spin. Heat rises from the ground, seeping into me until I and the earth are one. Closing my eyes, I listen to the ticking, tickling, soft scratching of hidden creatures busy about their day. My body is completely relaxed, my bones almost pliable, bending into the shape of the ground beneath me.

At last I get up, still a little dizzy, and I am slow to put on my rucksack, so I stand for a while, just gazing around.

I can see forever.

The horizon rolls away over the edge of the world, the ploughed earth is a patchwork of squares of ochre, umber, raw sienna, marking out fields like a quilt. Most of the crops have been harvested, and the track I start to follow weaves in and around, sometimes falling into a gentle dip which hides smiling sunflowers nodding as I pass by. The rich smell of recently ploughed soil pervades, and I stoop to pick up a lump of yellow clay, slowly crumbling it between my fingers. I consider how it might be used for a different crop – platters, bowls, figurines from the hands of a potter, perhaps. What colour would it be, after the trauma of the kiln's fire? I think it could be anything from cream to brown to terracotta red. I am tempted to mix a little piece with water to test its plasticity, but it's too hot to waste any water, so I watch it fall through my fingers, like saying good bye to a friend.

There are dry ditches between the track and the fields, full of wild flowers, butterflies, beetles, and other treasures. Surprisingly, for such a dry place, snails cluster up stems of wild grasses, their shells multicoloured spirals of pink, yellow, green and black. From time to time, a light wind blows through the dry grass, making a faint rattle, and I wonder is it the sound of the seed pods scattering the remnants of seeds, or the snail shells bumping against each other.

I catch a glimpse of the next village in the distance, almost two hours walk away, and I feel a little tired. A cup of tea would be very nice. A tiny butterfly wobbles past, landing on the vegetation, and I soon forget being tired – it's a purple hairstreak! In my haste to get my camera, I frighten it away, but another one comes along, and poses for a second. Got it!

The clanking sound of machinery behind me heralds the approach of a tractor, and I expect it will pass by, but it stops. The young driver alerts me to the news that swarms of angry hornets, not native to here, are on their way. I thank him, and he drives away, leaving me wondering if I should have asked for a lift. Is this why I didn't see anyone else walking all day? I take precautionary measures. I have a piece of fine netting at the bottom of my rucksack which is usually used on doorways to keep out flies, and I have seldom had to use it, but now it is a godsend. I drape it over my head like a burkha, fixing it in place with my sunhat. Then I put on long trousers, tucking the net into the waist band, keeping my arms covered.

I hear them before I see them.

A faint buzzing becomes a loud drilling sound, angry and threatening, and now I am bombarded with spiteful little missiles hitting the netting, trying to locate a way to my quivering skin. Ridiculously, I swing my stick about, getting as angry as they are, hearing a splat as I connect with some. I keep walking fast and I yell at them, swinging the stick wildly. Suddenly, they disappear, and I am relieved. There's nothing else I can do but keep on moving, and soon the next contingent arrives. It must look comical, if there is anyone here to see me leaping about, swinging my stick, clad in a bunch of mosquito netting, swearing loudly.

After a couple more assaults, they all seem to have passed, and miraculously I manage to avoid being stung. I keep the netting on though, until I am almost in the next village.

Sitting in the sun, outside the only bar in the village, drinking tinto al verano. That's rose wine with lemonade and crushed strawberries, says the barman, as he places another jug on the table, and the dozen or so pilgrims relaxing there don't argue, it's delicious whatever it is. I hold out my glass for a refill, the ice cubes tumbling with a splash along with the wine.

The camino route goes straight through the village, along the one street there is, and it takes about four minutes to walk from one end of the village to the other. We have been watching the pilgrims passing through, calling out a slightly slurred 'Buen Camino' to them, and occasionally our greeting tempts one or two to join us. The barman is happy because he can leave the job of drumming up custom to us.

As usual, conversation is lively, and the question always comes up – why are you walking the camino? At this time of the afternoon, and with a large measure of alcohol being involved, we are getting to the silly stage, giggling at everything, toasting one another and attempting to sing each other's national anthems. Suddenly, a tall blond man, who had said little up to now, begins to sob loudly, shoulders heaving, tears streaming down his face. He is quite sincere as he tells of his troubles and at first, everyone listens, trying not to laugh. His deadpan expression as he talks, the waterfall of tears that he is able to turn on and off at will, his hand continually sneaking out for more bread – and the fact that he is very, very drunk make him seem so funny.

"My wife is a very clever woman" he declares. He pronounces it 'vife'. He has a very loud voice, and he shouts his answer to any question put to him.

"She is a psychologist, you know, a real one. Yeah".

He nods to himself. “Yeah”. He says again. He gives the appearance of being about to doze off, then bursts out,

“My wife, she is sick of me, she has sent me on this walk to find myself. How can I do that? I don’t know who I’m looking for, because I don’t know who I am. What? You think I’m crazy? So does she. She says that she cannot cure me. What? No, she will not try anymore, she has sended – what? Oh, sorry, she has sent- is this correct? I don’t know how to speak sometimes. Yes, so many doctors, but still I am not made better. Hey, are you telling me I be drunk? I am not drunk, you are insulting me!”.

He struggles to get up from his chair, looking threatening, but only manages to topple over. He is hauled upright, and continues as though nothing has happened. I study him from a safe distance, noting that he seems to have no rucksack, his expensive looking shoes show no sign of recent use on rough ground, and he has a fat wallet on the table in front of him. I think he is about thirty-five, and is possibly Swedish. Someone enquires about the nature of his illness.

“I am sad” he says mournfully. “So sad for the world, so much sorrow. It is so terrible to see so much bad times for peoples, and I cannot fix it. It makes me depressed. My wife, she does not like depressed. She says I only marry her because she is rich. She says I don’t want to be better, because I don’t want to work.”

He sniggers, looking like a sly schoolboy, and says,

“Maybe this is a little bit true, but she is very rich. Why should I work?”.

Later on, the street empties as we go to whichever albergue we have earlier checked into, and our Swedish friend disappears in a taxi, having more stylish accommodation in mind. He is having a different kind of camino. At the albergue I am staying in, twenty-two pilgrims sit each side of a long dining table, having eaten a superb paella prepared by the couple who own this place. Tonight, we are invited to share our camino experiences so far with each other and also with the people who live in this community. People keep on piling into the room, as though there is a performance about to take place. I suppose there is, in a way. Our host speaks only Spanish, but he has devised a sort of programme, and makes a valiant effort to help us get to know a little about each other, asking us in turn to say where we are from and what work we do. The local population are also to do the same. This is hilarious, becoming a sort of international charades, and it’s an entertaining way to overcome the lack of a common language.

When it's my turn, I am reluctant to say 'retired', as though I am idle, so I say, for the first time in my life, "I am an artist". I've never said that out loud before, and I feel a bit of a fraud. I manage to say that in Spanish, and immediately, everything gets a bit crazy.

Our host shouts,

"My friend is an artist, he is here! Pedro, where are you? "

Everyone starts looking for him, then someone says he is still at his house. Our host fights his way through the throng out into the street, running up the road, calling "Pedro! Pedro!" at the top of his voice. He hasn't far to go, and is soon back with his friend in tow, a tall shy middle-aged man, who seems quite embarrassed by the attention. I am brought into the private sitting room of the owners, and shown some of his work. Others pile in, privacy abandoned, and the lovely delicate watercolour paintings are really beautiful. I am asked what do I paint, so I show some photos I had taken on my camera to Pedro. The camera is snatched from my hands as soon as Pedro is finished looking at them, and passed round, people flicking through the images until the batteries run down.

Pedro and I are obliged to stand together while a queue forms , all wanting to have their photograph taken with two 'famous' artists. I think Pedro felt just as reluctant as I did, but it was too late to refuse. And anyway, it is the first time, and probably the last, that I will ever be called famous!

A serious party develops, and I try, but I just can't stick the pace. I quietly slip away to my bunk, and I fall asleep, happy to have been famous, even if it is for one night only.

PART FOURTEEN

JOSE, ANTON, MARIA AND ME.

Next morning, as we leave, we are informed that there are robbers in the area, and it would be best not to travel alone. I wonder if the two men who performed tricks and acrobatics in the street yesterday are being referred to. They are ragged, thin and not too clean, with a starved-looking dog who can disappear for an hour or two, returning discreetly with a hen, or a big piece of butter or a potato. I have been talking to them, and find they are from a rural area of Poland, and they hope to reach England someday. They have no money, no maps, nothing at all except the dog, and are relying totally on the kindness of strangers. Last night, the villagers had been a little disapproving when some of us gave the men some food, saying that they are not true pilgrims, and we should not encourage them, but I think they are real and true. I and my fellow pilgrims have planned our journey, packed our rucksacks, made sure our boots are in good repair, and have the luxury of taking a flight to wherever we want to start, and money to pay for a bed each night. We are self-reliant.

They have nothing. They are reliant on God.

Today, I have company. As I am leaving the albergue, a woman rushes over to me, throwing her arms around me theatrically, hugging me far too tightly for a complete stranger. I instinctively clamp my arm firmly over my money pouch, while she cries on my shoulder. She is convinced that we have met some years ago on the camino, and fate has brought us together again. She tucks her arm into mine, calling out to everyone that we are long lost sisters.

Well, I don't remember her. Gently, I disengage my arm and try to say that perhaps she may have the wrong person, but she is convinced that we have met before. A thin, dark man, Jose, has been translating for her, and I ask him some questions. He tells me that he has only just met her. Her name is Maria, she is middle-eastern, and speaks only her own language. He says he doesn't know what language it is, but he speaks it too, obviously, so he must know. She lives in Bilbao. A woebegone youth of about 20 years is walking with them, he does not want to walk alone. He speaks perfect English, and has dropped out of university. He is very aware of his parent's disappointment. His name is Anton. He is from Toledo.

I start walking, and Maria once more takes my arm, walking closely beside me. Jose and Anton are deep in conversation, a little way behind.

"Maria, I can't walk like this. We are out of step with each other. Let go, please."

She pretends not to understand, but I insist. She cries, she berates me for not caring for her, even though it is a miracle we have met again, but, I insist. Jose says,

"Why does it matter? If you just let her walk with you, she will be happy. Why not?"

But I push her firmly away, saying,

"I cannot walk like this, and I really want to walk alone."

Then I stride away quickly, before she can cling on to me again. For a while, I can hear her toiling along behind me, but I don't look back. Then a faint voice calls,

"It is God's will that we met, and He will make us meet again. Goodbye, my sister".

This time, I look back. She is standing still, tears pouring down her cheeks, waving to me and trying to smile. I feel that I have overreacted, and so I wait until she catches up with me. She is tired, cold and hungry and I am cold too, so we stop to put on some extra layers and have something to eat. Jose and Anton arrive, and we enjoy each other's company – Jose has a fund of stories about life in rural Spain. Perhaps I have allowed myself to become too solitary, so I just let myself go and enjoy the craic. On our right, tall, elegant wind turbines wave indolently, and Maria and I run around in circles, arms outstretched, screaming like children pretending to be Don Quixote tilting at windmills, almost airborne on the strong wind.

Jose walks with me for a time, telling me that Anton suffers from depression, and has tried to commit suicide once. His doctor suggested that he might find healing by walking the camino, but so far he has not found peace. Jose tells me nothing about himself.

Below us, hidden in a fold in the land, is the village of Hontanas. We hear it before we see it, the sound of voices rising into the ether until at last we arrive, flopping gratefully down onto creaking wicker chairs. Coffee and croissants are put before us and we eat and talk happily to other pilgrims gathered there. A tall, handsome man from Bulgaria asks if he may have some of our croissants, and we say 'of course'. He tells us that he was in the albergue when Pedro and I were getting our photographs taken. Then, without asking permission, he reaches over and takes my camera, looking through the images until he finds the one he wants. He puts it flat on the table and takes a photograph, saying smugly,

"Other people pay for this, I get it free!"

Then he gathers up his belongings and off he goes. It happens so fast that I don't stop him, and I am annoyed with myself. I can't believe that I just sat there and did nothing.

We do not spend much more time in Hontanas, and are soon under way again. We marvel at the fields of sunflowers, the insects darting in and out among them, birds often in pursuit, and the breath-taking height of the sky above. Maria starts to sing, and I listen to her rich deep voice, not daring to join in. Jose tries too, but her voice is amazing so we just listen in awe. Anton is having a problem with blisters, so I stop to help him put some plasters on them to ease the discomfort. He asks me forlornly,

"Why are you always happy?"

I am totally stuck for words, the question is so unexpected. How can I answer? I stutter a banal reply, knowing it's not what he needs to hear, bending over his foot to avoid eye contact. I retreat into asking him why he is not able to be happy, but he doesn't know, he just never is, and never has been, not even as a child. He says that nothing has ever excited him, or made him laugh loudly, and the camino is just a long walk to be endured. I am profoundly sad to hear his thoughts, no glimpse of light in his inner darkness.

About four or five kilometres from Castrojeriz, the camino passes under the fourteenth century archway which vaults over the sharp bend in the road at the ruins of the Convent of San Anton. As we approach, Maria points to the Bulgarian we met in Hontanas, who is just ahead of us, limping badly. She calls out to him, and he pauses, which probably saves his life. A car hurtles round the bend, loses control, and sails into the air, right over our heads, coming to rest on its side in a stubble field. There's a long drop into the field and we rush to help, Maria scorning to waste time, launching herself into the field in one leap. This is no tiny Irish field, it's a proper Spanish one, so by the time we get to the car, steaming gently on its side, the driver has absconded. The passenger is reeling and stumbling around the field as though he is drunk, hotly pursued by Maria, shouting,

"Wait! Wait! I am a nurse!"

She never mentioned that before.

A police van arrives, and myself and a few other pilgrims describe what has happened. I look around for Maria and Jose, but they seem to have vanished, only Anton is here. Then I suddenly remember something. When I asked Maria to let go of my arm earlier today, she replied in Spanish, and also when she chased the passenger around the field, she used Spanish. I wonder what that's all about.

After the police have gone, I check into the nearest albergue, but Anton moves on to another one which is at the end of this long village. I am glad, as I need some space between myself and them. The rest of the afternoon I spend in washing my clothes, a daily routine as I have only one change of clothes with me. Then I wander around the streets, and I soon encounter Maria and Jose. Maria is very upset that I am staying in a different albergue, then she brightens up, saying,

"Come and eat with us at our albergue, come at seven."

By seven o'clock, I am ravenous, and standing outside their albergue. They greet me and Jose announces

"Now we go to buy something to eat – Pauline, you can buy the tomatoes, the bread, the wine – "

"Yes" I say quickly and so we go. To a bar. We talk, we drink, we talk, and talk. By eight o'clock, I am faint with hunger, and at last, we go into a shop and buy our food. Back at their albergue, there is a queue for the cooker. So we wait, we drink, we talk, they talk, I can't talk any more, I'm too hungry. At last, it's our turn at the cooker, and finally, we eat. It's 9.50pm. My albergue is one kilometre away.

Lights go out at 10pm.

Next morning, I have a slow start to the day, but Jose, Maria and Anton are waiting for me outside their albergue, so off we go, soon making heavy going of the steep climb out of Castrojeriz. It is still dark, but as we reach the top of Alto de Mostelares, and look back, golden light is suffusing the early morning mist, and Castrojeriz is shimmering like a magical fairytale city. We stay a little while, quiet, watching light spreading into the valley below, then we turn and walk, saying nothing.

I think it is time to part company with Maria, Jose and Anton. I really never intended to walk with the same people every day, I prefer to go at my own pace without the pressure of being tied to certain times or places. And truthfully, Maria's very intense clinging and her insistence that I go to Fromista with them is becoming irksome. I resolve to make the break when we reach Itero de la Vega. We stop for coffee, and I am about to tell them that I'm going on, but before I have a chance, Jose takes me to one side and says in a low voice,

"I have a proposition for you."

Quickly I reply "I'm not interested", but Jose is very pushy, and says "Just listen before you decide".

My answer is that I put on my rucksack, lift my stick and start to walk away. Maria gives a little squeal of dismay and runs after me, protesting loudly. Now I am seriously annoyed, and I stop dead. I say,

“This part of the camino is very special to me, and I need to be alone.”

“But what about Fromista?”

“No Fromista”.

Loud wails fail to move me and at last I feel free again as I leave, not looking back. I wonder why she was so keen to stop in Fromista? Then it occurs to me that perhaps the robbers we were warned about are not the two Polish guys with their dog, but a couple who seem overly keen to go to Fromista.

PART FIFTEEN

PARADISE.

There is nobody in sight, the empty track snaking away into the distance, and in the vegetation along the ditch everything is moving and whirring, clicking and chewing. The vast stubble fields on each side of the track are golden, with a few bright red poppies here and there. I am almost dancing along, punching the air with my fist, shouting into the sky,

"Thank you, thank you!"

I look as though I am crazy, and I probably am, this is sheer heaven all around me and I can't drink it in fast enough. Ochre dust particles hang in the air, light reflecting off so that it seems the sky is yellow. The heat is overpowering, and I slow down, so other pilgrims begin to overtake me. There is no shelter, but I am high as a kite, totally in love with this land. I don't want this to stop, I want to walk on and on and on, into forever. My boots, my socks and lower legs are all the same shade of yellow ochre, coated with fine soft dust. I don't want to wash it off, I want to keep it like that, a tangible piece of this day.

At the edge of the village of Boadilla del Camino, there is a fountain which looks as though it has been dry for a long time, surrounded by a low stone wall. I sit down, only noticing now that my feet are burning, my ankles aching from the stony ground. There is no shelter, but I am content to sit, thinking dreamily of the last few wonderful kilometres. There is an albergue right beside the fountain, and other pilgrims begin to gather there. When will the albergue open? They push themselves into a queue of sorts, but I can't be bothered so I stay sitting, dreaming.

Suddenly, the door flies open and a crazy-looking guy hurtles out, stumbles, almost falling at my feet. He recovers himself, stands up straight, replaces his hat and yells at me,

"What do you want?"

"A bed" I say, and he nods.

Then he says sharply,

"I am cleaning, you wait one hour. One hour you wait"

"I wait" I reply.

The pilgrim queue begins to crowd around the door, shoving and pushing in a most un-pilgrim like way. He pushes them aside, screaming,

"Go away! You can't come in! This is not the albergue with the Olympic swimming pool. Go away!".

A Norwegian woman manages to squeeze past, trying to advance up the path leading to a hidden garden. But he shoves her out, yelling,

"This is not the albergue with the Olympic swimming pool! You only want to look because you want the best – you are not a real pilgrim. Go away! You can't come in!"

He lunges at the other pilgrims, swinging a stick wildly, and they move hastily away. I sit on the wall, waiting. He grabs my arm and pulls me through the door, closing it with a crash behind us.

We enter the Garden of Eden.

Fig trees, apples, pears, lemons, grapes, all heavy with fruit against the white painted walls, flowers mixed with peppers, courgettes, tomatoes, beans, oh a whole cornucopia of fresh, fresh foods. Trees sway gently in the hot breath of the meseta, there's a hammock, some chairs and tables, green lawns well-tended, and……………..a swimming pool. Not an Olympic sized one, but bigger than the one at the other side of the village. Nice irony.

"What is your name?" he demands.

I tell him.

"Oh!" he says, "I will call you Mac".

As the afternoon wears on, he screams abuse at the pilgrims rattling the door. Just once, he asks a few questions, then drags a young Canadian girl in. Her name is Riley, and she is a carpenter by trade. He pours a cool beer for each of us, then we wander after him, a huge elderly hound of unknown ancestry bringing up the rear. He takes us through his garden, naming each plant and shrub. He is especially proud of his herbs, and we discuss the various uses they have, both culinary and medicinal. He is serene in his garden, smoking as we go around, talking through the fragrance.

Next, we are shown where we will sleep tonight. This is a small albergue, with a couple of private rooms also on offer. It is a very basic place, but everything is spotless – floors, showers, kitchen all sparkling clean. He tells us that he doesn't want too many pilgrims, they make the place dirty and don't clean up after themselves. The kitchen is not to be used for frying, in fact he would rather it wasn't used at all. We can choose where we wish to sleep, and we both opt for a private room each. They are Spartan and cell –like, but cool, and we settle in, taking care to clean the showers thoroughly after use.

Then it's back out to the garden, me hoisted somehow into the hammock.

More beer. More smoke.

"Mac, you are queen of this albergue, tonight you do nothing. Just relax. We will cook....Riley from Canada, can you cook?"

About two hours later, a very burnt, inedible omelette appears, with nothing else. We stare at it, then offer it to the dog, who turns away in disgust. Then we all burst out laughing, and turn back to the beer. I do wonder why the produce in the garden is not used, but this is not a rational situation and questions might offend, so I just sip my beer and forget my empty stomach. And anyway, I'm soooo relaxed! Canada, Ireland and Spain, playing dominoes, talking nonsense all evening, smoke curling and swirling slowly. He says,

"A pilgrim must have humility, patience and adaptation". I say,

"the camino gives so much, some for your life, some for sharing, and some for letting go".

We nod sagely, imagining we are profound.

Goodnight.

The morning is cool, and at six, Riley and myself are ready to leave. There is no sign of life apart from the dog, so we leave without saying goodbye. Two sticks are propped against the door, with a scrap of paper saying 'Take one', so we do, then pulling the door behind us, shut ourselves out of the Garden of Eden forever.

PART SIXTEEN

A LITTLE DETOUR.

I've always wanted to sleep in a teepee. Not the kind I made as a child, with brushes and walking sticks precariously tethered together with a skipping rope, and a sheet draped over, but a real teepee. One that didn't collapse as my younger brothers tried to crawl in after me, one that had intricate designs on the outside, and a real fire just beside it, so that I could sit in the opening and smoke a pipe, a tall feather in my hair.

It looks as though my childhood dream is about to come true. After passing swiftly through Fromista, I take a little detour, then I slow my pace to a dawdle, enjoying the quiet morning. After a few pleasant kilometres, I come upon a small village, with a sign on the right indicating an albergue. The track I am on is a little higher than the houses, and I look down to see a large field with four teepees, a gypsy caravan and some buildings, including a bar. 'That will do nicely' I think, and I scramble across a ditch, clambering up just opposite the bar. There seems to be a crisis of identity here, as besides the Indian teepees, the Romany caravan, the Spanish bar, there is a Caribbean overtone with coconut trees (artificial), colourful bunting and a girl coming to meet me wearing a grass skirt.

I begin to enquire about the accommodation, but she says I can have a drink first, there's no need to hurry, it's early, I am the only customer. Indeed, I am, as it's only twelve thirty, and too early to stop walking for the day. She puts a pineapple cocktail on the table, waving my offer of payment away. It has two paper umbrellas and a chunk of pineapple in it and one sip later I agree, there's no hurry, no hurry at all.

Sipping my drink, eyes half closed, sun beating down, how relaxed can this be? I am definitely staying here tonight. I doze off for a minute or two, so I don't notice a posse of inquisitive donkeys' approach from behind me, until a quivering, slobbery nose sneezes mightily down my back, and nearly blows me off my chair. I finish my drink, closely attended by the posse, then the girl appears again, telling me to pick anywhere I want….teepee, caravan, tent that is not quite a yurt nor a tent, or a long, spacious albergue with every facility needed.

Eagerly I head for the teepee, the patter of tiny hooves close behind. Alas, this is not for me, as it is almost as badly made as those of my childhood. It is cramped and suffocatingly hot, with the walls billowing loosely so that they press inward, like an air bag in a car that has been inflated. The caravan is too dark – how fussy am I? So the posse and I head over to inspect the albergue, skipping the yurt/tent. As we pass the bar, the girl tells me that it was once the donkeys' quarters, and to make sure to shut the door behind me, as they may try to follow me in.

Indeed, they do. After much shoving and pushing, I manage to secure the door, and turn to survey a long kitchen, decorated in bright Mexican style, with a seating area at the end. A door leads to two huge dormitories and newly installed very modern shower rooms, all sparkling clean. Oh yes, this is for me.

I take my time in choosing a bunk, rather smug as I am first, so I get the best bed. I take time to shower, then it's off to the bar for a light lunch and another cocktail or two.

All day long, pilgrims come – and go. By six thirty, I am not so smug, there's nobody in the albergue except me. Surely I don't smell? I've had a shower. There's only so much people- watching a person can do, and it's worse when there isn't any people there to watch. Around seven, dinner is served, a communal meal but on this occasion with no company. The food is delicious, and I take my time, then off to bed early, with a truth I don't wish to acknowledge – sometimes, solitude can be downright boring.

The day is not done with me yet. I had closed the door carefully, conscious of the donkeys being somewhat put out by my occupation of their former abode, but they are smarter than the average donkey. Around midnight, four of them march confidently up between the rows of empty bunks, their hooves skittering on the newly tiled floor. They halt by my bunk, and stand staring, waiting. Maybe they are trying to stare me out, and think I will leave, but I have history with donkeys, and I briskly usher them out, past the showers, through the kitchen and out the door. They begin to hammer on the door, one emitting a loud, long bray, which I'm inclined to believe contained indignant donkey swear words. I fire off a few choice words back, then I turn to find a frightened looking man cowering behind me, a walking stick held in his shaking hand. Almost as shaky as mine is at times.

"Where did you come from?" I bark at him. "Where were you all evening?"

He clearly doesn't speak English, and scuttles off to the other dormitory, closing the door quickly against strange donkey herding, swearing, Irish women. He shouldn't be let out on his own.

PART SEVENTEEN

A REAL PILGRIM.

He is standing along the track leading into Carrion de los Condes, looking thinner than ever. There is no sign of his companion or their dog. I say nothing as I pass by, nor do I make eye contact with him. I am feeling sorry for myself because I am tired, and wishing to wallow in self-pity, have selfishly none left for others. I find an albergue which is located in a former convent, and listlessly check in. It is positively luxurious, a huge, light, airy room with beds, not bunks, each with a chair and a locker beside them. I begin to cheer up, my aches and pains soothed by a long, hot shower. Then I sally forth to find something to eat.

Strolling along at my leisure, I meet many of the people I had encountered since the start of the camino, and it is such pleasure to meet again, comparing experiences, chatting, having a glass of wine. A tall English lady I had talked to along the way just today waves me over, inviting me to join her and her friends to eat. She left England, with her husband and children, to live in France, where they are hoping to open a bed and breakfast business. It is proving to be a much more complicated affair than they had thought, and it is becoming a struggle to keep going. She is a therapist, in reflexology and massage. Sadly, she finds the camino exhausting, and has made the decision to go home when she reaches Leon. I have a fleeting moment of smug self-satisfaction, thinking how fit I am, sure I could never give in like that.

I am really hungry. The tantalizing aromas emanating from the kitchen holds the promise of a tasty meal, and I can hardly wait. At last, the waiter brings our meals. I reach for some cutlery, and as I do so, a savage pain shoots up my back, and I fall back into my chair, the cutlery scattering over the table. I can barely move, and I bite deep into my lip to keep from screaming. My companions are upset, but I can't speak, all I can do is leave some money on the table and somehow get to the albergue.

This had happened to me once before, and it took weeks to recover from it. How am I going to manage this time? The English lady comes alongside me and somehow we make it to the albergue. I collapse onto the bed, tears of pain and disbelief burning down my cheeks. Through a haze of despair, I hear the instruction to lie face down, and with difficulty I do so. The English lady says nothing more, but for almost an hour, she works on my back until the pain recedes to a dull ache. She brings me a cup of tea, and then advises me to take a rest day tomorrow, but for now, just sleep.

Morning arrives, and to my astonishment, I have no pain at all. I look around to see if anyone is left, but there is just one young man, who is softly playing a guitar. I lie back on the bed, listening to the familiar strains of 'Recuerdos de Alhambra' and trying to decide what to do. Eventually I have a plan. I will take a taxi to Calzadilla de la Cueza, rest there for a day, then hopefully continue the camino from there.

The taxi rank is in a café near a busy junction, and I struggle to make myself heard above the noise of the traffic. At last, I manage to arrange a taxi. I am told it is too early now but he will be here in an hour. That's okay.

Being quite near the place where the camino exits the town, I wander along, just to fill up the hour I must wait for the taxi. I gaze up the path, wondering if I could change my mind and chance walking, but the more prudent me says 'no'. A tap is attached to a post which is buried in a grassy bank, with a notice warning there is no water, shade or facilities between here and the next village, 17 kilometres away. I am about to move on, when I see the Polish man that I ignored yesterday, lying on the grass, shivering. I am suddenly aware and ashamed of my behavior then, conscious of the contrast of the care taken of me, while he appears to be invisible to all who pass by.

"Are you okay?" He is startled by my voice and immediately begins to apologise, neither of us knowing why. I assure him that I only want to ask if he is alright, so he tells me he has a sore foot.

"Can I see?" He reluctantly shows me – and it is a mess. Most of his foot resembles raw meat, red and lurid. Pus oozes from several places, and as he was walking in a pair of old flip flops, there was no chance of it healing. He has urged his friend to keep on walking, while he hopes for something to happen to allow him to carry on, too. I delve into my rucksack for my first aid kit, which I have not had to use for myself so far. I also find my towel and soap. As gently as possible, I wash the foot a few times until there is no pus or blood seeping out. I dry it well, and apply plasters, antiseptic cream and tcp where necessary. I have a bottle of dry antibiotic which I liquidize with water from the tap, telling him how to use it, hoping he understands my mimed instructions.

Well, I can't walk away from this yet, can I? So I offer to share the taxi ride with him, assuring him that I will be paying. He is so happy, but the taxi man isn't, though. On the pale cream upholstery, several tiny black dots jump about, and I struggle to stop myself from scratching.

A couple of days later, I see the man for the last time. He is across the street with his friend, but he spots me and dives into the traffic. He makes it safely to where I am, and proudly shows me how well his foot is now. Today, he wears a flip flop on one foot, and a discarded running shoe on the other, and is as happy a man as anyone. I, on the other hand, am well rewarded for my selfishness, self-satisfaction and neglect with multiple stinging, itching bites, that ooze disgustingly for the next couple of days.

PART EIGHTEEN

STAINED GLASS AND SANDALS.

Road works, road works, road works. Coming into the city of Leon, on a hot, hot afternoon, I manage to lose the way. There are so many red cones and signs that somehow, the yellow arrows are nowhere to be seen, the pavements ripped up, leaving me thoroughly confused. I plod along, hoping and praying for some sign of my location. Aha, there's a sign saying albergue. I follow it, but it leads me around in a huge circle right back to where I was. When I first arrived in the city, I was not in distress, just a little tired, but now I'm feeling quite sick. I need to stop. I sit down on some steps, in the shade of a church which is peculiarly built on a corner, with a path for pedestrians running through it. Some small boys ask me if I need anything, so I give them five euros and tell them to bring me water. They disappear, but soon come back with the water, and a nun in a grey habit, who says she will take me to the albergue. I try to give the children a few coins, but they shyly shake their heads, running off to play again.

The nun takes me through a maze of streets and I know I could never have found my way alone. Yet again, I am being looked after by total strangers who could just as easily ignored me – but they didn't. The dormitory is large, dark, noisy and crowded. I lie down, on a thin, uncomfortable mattress, and the bunk above me seems to be very close to my face. If someone takes the upper bunk it will be too claustrophobic for me. There is no chance to sleep, and so I sit up, banging my head on the metal frame of the bunk. A commotion starts in the far corner, and I go over to investigate. On the edge of a bed, a woman sits, her leg, which is encased in plaster, extended in front of her. She is complaining most piteously that someone brought her sandwiches instead of pizza, and she wants tea, not coffee. A young girl is trying to placate the woman, but she is loud and angry, swearing at all and sundry. It seems most ungrateful, and then she shouts even louder.

"Where the hell is that stupid girl who is getting me my ticket to Paris?"

Someone standing behind me says she has been here for the last six days, having tripped and broken her ankle getting off a bus. She is ordering anyone who passes to look after her, including taking her to hospital daily by taxi, bringing her food, doing her washing, making arrangements for her to travel to Paris. She says that she has no money left, so other pilgrims are paying for this, but she doesn't care if they can afford it or not. She never says please or thank you. She is Australian, (sorry, Australia!) but though her insurance should probably pay for a flight home, she has decided to go to Paris to stay with some people she met a few years ago but hasn't seen since. She has a phone number for these unfortunate would be hosts, and has been ringing constantly but a recorded message says they are away on holiday. This does not deter her, she's going to turn up on their doorstep anyway.

I would like to recount her complaints as I heard them, but as it consists mostly of expletives, it's pointless, it's not even remotely funny. A harassed looking girl with beautiful red curly hair comes in, and the woman demands the ticket. The girl tries to explain that there is more than one ticket involved as there's no direct flight to Paris, but the tickets are thrown up in the air, and the girl bursts into tears. There is an embarrassed silence, then someone takes the girl away, a comforting arm around her, while a stout Danish woman takes charge, and the situation calms down. A whip round gathers enough money to pay back the red-haired girl who had paid the woman's fare out of her own money, leaving herself short of enough to complete the camino, so that's good. Even better, the woman's journey starts tonight, so a taxi is ordered before she can protest, and her belongings are swiftly packed, the taxi arrives and at last, she's gone.

I am not sure that I want to stay in this albergue. It's just too busy. I make a quick decision, pack up again, and leave. I walk towards the city centre, this time following the arrows without any difficulty, and chance upon a small hotel close to the cathedral. The price is a bit more than I expected but I check in anyway – for three nights. What's going on?

The truth is, I'm tired. And I'm not nice when I'm tired. I haven't even been singing, so it's time to stop for a while to rest and reflect.

Rest first. I am shown to my room, a tiny attic with a velux window, from which it is just possible to glimpse a view over the rooftops, to …some more rooftops! It's a lovely little hideaway, and I hurry into the shower before I sink into a cool, downy little bed. There's a fridge, well stocked, and I reach for the white wine. Then I sit up in bed, sipping my wine, reading, dozing, passing a very pleasant evening. I am on holiday from myself, and already I am calmer, now that the pressure to keep moving is off. I'll think about things tomorrow – or the next day.

Next morning starts off cool, and I am up and about early. Breakfast is served on the street, a row of tables from various hotels busy coming and going. I am leafing through a sheaf of information on what to do in Leon, when a gentle voice enquires 'may I join you?' It is Gerhardt, a fellow pilgrim, and I say 'of course'. Over breakfast, we decide to visit some art galleries, then perhaps view the famous stained-glass windows in the cathedral. Gerhardt is good company, and the day slips by easily. We meet the English lady who attended to my back, she will be leaving in the morning to return to France by train. We agree to meet later for dinner, then part company to rest before our meal. I think I could live like this every day!

Later, I hurry along towards the restaurant where we agreed to meet, colliding with a tall, stout man I had walked with some days previously. He invites himself along, and that's ok as we are all acquainted already. As we walk,

I am aware of him observing me closely, but he was a policeman before he retired so I think nothing of it, it is probably the habit of a lifetime of observation.

Then, he puts a hand on my arm to slow us down, and peers into my face, saying,

"You have only one."

Immediately I know what he is referring to. I had a mastectomy a few years ago, but I'm not particularly conscious of my appearance, so I am not wearing a false breast, and anyway, it's uncomfortable in the heat. I say,

"Yes, but what does it matter? I don't care about that."

Then he tells me that his partner had a mastectomy four years ago, but she is so distressed and ashamed that she won't go out of their house, and won't allow him in their bed in case he sees her as she is. He is very sad. He can't find a way to comfort her, and in despair he has come to walk the camino, hoping to gain some peace for both of them. I think, how sad that she survived from cancer, but can't escape from a prison of her own making. He stands still, trying to get control of his emotions, and I realize that there are two victims in this story. How sad, also, for a surgeon who operated skillfully on her, only to realize that it didn't bring joy or new life to the couple.

At last, he is able to continue to our meeting place. There is an Indian restaurant that I am keen to try, so Gerhardt agrees to come with me, while the others go to get some tapas. We make a good choice. There is music playing discreetly in the background, the décor is rich and colourful, and the food looks absolutely delicious.

It is early, so there is only one other table occupied. They are a Spanish couple, about twenty-eight to thirty years old. The man seems very tense and impatient, drumming his fingers on the table, looking around him and making remarks, and being extremely rude to the waiter. From where we are seated, we have a clear view, and we pity the waiter who has to endure such abuse. They have finished their first course, and the next course is brought to them. Strips of beef in an aromatic sauce, served sizzling hot on a metal plate. I think I might have that, too, it looks so appetizing.

The man stares at his plate for a few seconds, then screams at the waiter.

"This is shit! It's not fit to eat. Are you trying to poison me? It's shit!"

The waiter has no time to reply, as the man stands up and, gripping the edge of the table, overturns it onto the floor with a crash, hot food, glasses, cutlery flying everywhere. He swipes the tablecloth off a few more tables on his way out, with the woman hurrying after him, and puts his foot through a glass door panel as a parting gift, still screaming,

"This is shit!"

There is a shocked silence. Then the waiter asks if we are alright. Assuring him that there's no cause for concern, Gerhardt and I join in the cleaning up with the rest of the staff. At last we are finished. Now we pretend that everything is normal and order the rest of our meal. Much as I would like to, I resist the urge to order the beef and black bean sizzler. After our meal, we have a discussion with the waiter about what happened. It is not the first incident they have experienced. He asks us sadly,

"Is this good food? Maybe it is not good enough. Is it really so bad?"

Actually, it's one of the best meals I've had since starting the camino, and we assure him that it's really great. Our conversation eventually leads to the number of Indian restaurants in Dublin and how Irish people love Indian food. We are too late to meet with our friends, so the waiter locks up, and we stay on, having an impromptu party of sorts, when we solve all the problems of the world. Despite the unpleasant incident earlier, it turns into a lovely, memorable evening. We book a table for tomorrow night.

My second free day in Leon sees me up and out early again, and I stand in front of a shop, gazing longingly at a display of shoes. I don't need shoes, I have no room in my rucksack for shoes, I have no money for shoes – but oh boy, I am tempted. I have found a street that has nothing but shoe shops, and if I don't tear myself away NOW, I am liable to make a considerable dent in my camino budget. I distract myself with the thought of waffles and syrup, and I buy a sticky fist full from a street stall. Across the street there is a bench with a man sitting on one end, so I dodge the traffic and sit down beside him. He doesn't mind.

When I've finished, I lick the syrup from my fingers, and try to clean my hands with tissue, leaving little white tufts of it still clinging to me. I stare at the man sitting beside me, then I run my hand up his arm, over his face, his head – he doesn't mind. He is made of bronze. His name is Antoni Gaudi.

Today, Gerhardt is resting, the English lady is on her way home and the policeman is walking on, so I am free to think about the journey so far. I am not walking this camino to 'find myself', I know myself only too well. I'm hoping to change my old self and hopefully become a better self. And, to learn more about the God who lets bad things happen to good people, and lets good things happen to bad people.

I am always telling people never to miss an opportunity to help or share with others, no matter how trivial it may seem, but do I take my own advice? In Viana, was it really necessary to argue over a bunk bed? Or in Burgos, to speak so condescendingly to the doorman who was only doing his job? What about the hidden attitudes, my uncharitable thoughts to just about everyone in Puente de Reina? I seem to fall into the same old pattern of behavior, even though I know what 'love thy neighbour' means. It took two opportunities to prompt me to help that Polish man, because I put myself first, not wanting the bother.

I need to remember the difference between privilege and rights again. I need to remember that I have no right to judge anyone but myself. I need to realize that sharing everything also means sharing time. On this journey so far, I have been reminded of truths I had conveniently forgotten, so now I must move the focus of my life away from me, me, me. And I must not go back home with a load of platitudes that can be trotted out, to be used like sticking plasters to cover hurt.

I sit for a long time, dozing, thinking, dozing some more. The traffic is heavy, and all the noise of city life begins to seep into my consciousness. Suddenly, I feel restless, and in my mind I see the glorious blue sky of the meseta, feel the satisfying rhythm of walking on and on, the smell of the earth. I am ready to go on, and I am seized with impatience now. I need to be out of the city. I get up from the seat, say goodbye to Gaudi and go back to the hotel. I throw everything on the bed, and begin to pack for an early start tomorrow. It's only when I've finished that I remember Gerhardt and dinner.

At the restaurant, we are greeted like old friends, and there follows a delightful evening, with superb food, warm company and laughter. Strolling back to the hotel, Gerhardt confides that he must rest at least two more days. An accident some years ago left a legacy of a weak right knee, and it is very painful. The doctor advises him to stop, or at least rest a little longer. He is a shy person, and asks if I will wait for another few days, as he won't know anyone, those he made friends with will be too far ahead. I decline, feeling very awkward as I do so, not wanting to hurt his feelings. I tell him he will soon meet other people, but he is not convinced. He says a reluctant goodbye – goodbye forever. My last view of him is as he raises his arm to give a final farewell, then we both disappear from each other's sight.

PART NINETEEN

PAINTED EARTH.

I lie on my bunk in an albergue in El Acebo, eyes closed against the harsh florescent light in this dormitory. It is nearly ten o'clock, and all around me is the rustling, bustling of people getting ready for sleep before the lights go out. It's only a couple of days since I left Leon, and I feel that everything is going too fast, time slipping away relentlessly. I can't sleep yet, so to pass the time until its quieter, I begin to plan how I might portray on canvas the landscape I have fallen in love with, when I am home from the camino.

Up to now, 'home' has been a remote place, somewhere ahead. Now, as I realize that I am more than halfway along the camino, thoughts of being home slip into my mind from time to time.

I see myself sitting in front of a large blank canvas, recalling the stunning colours of the meseta. The sky, oh the sky is so many colours. It reflects the ochre earth particles suspended in the air, sharp lemon yellow or deep cadmium yellow. It can be the milky blue of morning, and I see myself mixing ultramarine with purest white, or at high noon, a vibrant cobalt blue. I watch myself hesitate, then I commit the brush to the canvas, confident of the picture in my mind. Colours named by someone long ago, like raw umber, burnt sienna, crimson, pale terracotta, venetian red, all on my palette.

Then the lights go out, and velvet darkness descends, allowing me to fall asleep, on the meseta once more in my dreams.

COLOURS.

I am in love with colours.

My eyes delight in shade and shadow,
Pale primrose yellow, bright buttercup,
Deep marigold, harsh lemon, bitter orange.

Ploughed earth of ochre, dark umber,
Smouldering burnt sienna under a fiery setting sun.
Copper beech leaves drifting,
Red maple, red berries,
Purple berries.

Innocent white hawthorn blossom
On a mild May morning,
Startling cobalt blue of a summer noontime sky,
Silent deep navy of a still, starry night.

Seashell pink, a baby's tiny fingernail,
Rose-pink flush of a sleeping curved cheek,
Soft, soft green of new grass,
Sharp, shiny holly, tall, dark pines.

Blue-black lumbering beetles,
Emerald sheen of a butterfly's wing.

PART TWENTY

LOST AGAIN.

I seem to have a habit of getting lost in towns and cities, either going in or going out. It's 7am and I lost the way out of Ponferrada at least half an hour ago. I stop, looking around for the familiar yellow arrows that should guide me out, but there's no sign of any. On my left is a huge car park, full to capacity, and on my right a line of shops and offices, all tightly closed and shuttered. There's no sign of life anywhere.

"Where are you from?"

A sharp voice calls out to me, as a youth of 18 or 20 years pops up from among the cars.

"Ireland". I reply, but I keep on walking. Two more young men appear from nowhere, one of them saying,

"We don't like Ireland. They beat Spain at football last night".

I don't reply, Ireland did indeed beat Spain last night. I keep on walking steadily, but they follow me, shouting,

"We don't like Ireland."

One of them shoves me on my back, and I stumble, recover, and march on. Another push. I turn to face them, swinging my trusty stick with its metal tip at them, my back against a wall. I can't hold them off too long. They are enjoying this, while I have visions of my rucksack being plundered, or worse. There is a piece of waste ground with a derelict building on it up ahead and they are herding me towards it, laughing, but I am determined not to let that happen. A shutter flies halfway up just beside me and I almost faint with relief. Quickly I duck underneath it. It's a bakery shop, the comforting smell of freshly baked bread enveloping me like a cloud of floury incense.

I ask for some croissants, and as I pay for them, my hands shake. I can't tell as I fumble for coins, dropping them, fiddling with my purse, clumsily counting them out, whether it's the upsetting circumstances that are causing it, or that irritating unnamed shake I've been carrying for a year or more.

Warily, I peer out. 'Oh good, they've gone'. I walk quickly away, a pulse hammering in my throat, my breath ragged and painful. I want to get away from here as fast as possible. I only cover a couple of hundred yards, when suddenly, they're back. They are serious now, and angry. Once again I swing my stick, striking one of them on his arm. He catches the end of the stick easily, and I can't wrest it from him. He slams me back against the wall with a shove, shouting into my face. I try not to look frightened, but my voice has dried up and I'm not able to squeak, never mind yell for help. I feel his breath on my face as he shouts again – then his face disappears, as all three of them take to their heels, running down an alleyway as fast as they can.

A pint-sized elderly lady with a poodle on a lead stands in an open doorway, furiously shaking her fist. She walks a little way down the alley after them, yelling shrilly. Her hair is dyed blue, and the poodle is also dyed the same colour. Every time she lifts her arm to shake her fist, she nearly chokes the poodle who dangles off the ground on his short lead. One of the young men is her grandson, and she calls curses down on him for all the shame and trouble he has caused in their family. She is going to tell his mother, though the shame will kill her, then he will be a murderer, Finally, she stops, and turns to survey this worm of a pilgrim. 'Why did I keep on walking when I realized I was lost? Have I no sense?' She takes the stupid pilgrim back down the street, round a few corners, then says, 'You are alright now – see, there's lots of other silly pilgrims', pointing at them trudging on their way.

She walks away without a backward glance, her spine straight as a ramrod, proud to have rescued a little of the family name.

I shuffle along, hardly able to move, but desperate to keep up with the straggle of pilgrims leaving the city. On a corner, a café has put some chairs and tables, making an early start to the day. I sink onto a chair, my legs weak and shaky. Tea and toast is what I need. At first, I sip slowly, and nibble at the toast, allowing myself to try thinking over what happened earlier, but I can't, my thoughts are all jumbled unpleasantly in my head. I am seized by the notion that they will come after me again, and I get to my feet, scrambling to put on my rucksack, pay for the tea and be off. I imagine the other pilgrims are walking faster than me, and I'm afraid to be left behind, so I end up running, my legs almost buckling under me, until I reach Fuente Nuevas.

This is ridiculous. I just can't allow this one upsetting experience to ruin what has been and still is, a wonderful journey. I will just have to get over myself.

Now.

I make myself deliberately walk slow, and gradually the pounding heartbeat and painful breathing subsides. I reason with myself, telling me that it is not likely to happen twice, it wasn't so bad, I didn't get hurt and anyway, I have a choice. I can go home, or keep on walking, what will it be? If I stay, I will have to put all thoughts of the incident out of my mind, at least until I do get home, otherwise it will be a waste of time, there would be no point in walking in a spirit of fear. It takes a few minutes, but then I come to a decision.

PART TWENTY-ONE

DECISION MADE.

Villafranca del Bierzo sits as though in a bowl amid the mountains. It's an enchanting town, with an aura of content remoteness, and I slow down inside and out as I walk through the quiet streets, the beautiful rose gardens, to the peaceful Plaza Major. I sit down at a café under the shelter of an archway and watch the rain, thunder rumbling in the distance. Two more pilgrims join me, they are Irish, and one carries a guitar, the other a couple of bongo drums. They cheerfully admit to taking the bus today, as they are running out of time, they have a flight to catch in a few days.

Once again, I am reminded of home. It seems a million miles away.

The musicians play and sing for a while, and soon the café is crowded, everyone enjoying the music and company. I fall into conversation with a woman from Latin America, a very deep-thinking person who listens with full attention when anyone else is speaking. As always, the question arises – why are you walking the camino? When she is asked, she gives a full and considered answer, saying,

"I have four sons and a husband, and I have never worked since I married, my husband preferred it that way. He is a very proud man. Before I was married, I worked in my father's jewellery business, designing. All my life so far, I have allowed my family to dictate how I live, first my father, then my husband, and now my teenage children also."

She pauses as more coffee comes, and I begin to think she will say nothing more, but then she continues,

"I had a dispute with my eldest son – he's eighteen – about his behaviour, and his attitude to me was arrogant and dismissive. I spoke to my husband, but I saw that he also talked to me as though I had no right to an opinion. This is my own fault, I have spoiled my family, but I am not willing to continue that way. I have my own money, I do not need to ask my husband for anything, so I decided to take time to think of how I wanted to live. I saw a travel programme about the camino, and here I am."

The guitar player asks,

"But did your husband not object to this?"

"Oh, he did object, he even tried to cancel my passport, my children think I am selfish, but my life has to change. Because I have changed, now I am not the same wife, not the same mother, not the same me. I am a free person. I need to live a real life."

"So, what happens next?" someone asks.

"I don't know. I have booked a hotel in Santiago for a week for my husband and myself. I have asked him to join me there when I finish this camino. I hope that I can explain to him how we need to live in a different way, and that he will accept this. But it might break my marriage if he cannot understand. He has not replied yet to me".

"What do you want to do?" the guitarist asks.

She shrugs, "Something real", she says.

The rain continues to pour down, but I want to have a siesta, so I walk in the warm, heavy rain, slowly getting very wet, to the albergue. A shower, a long restful siesta, then it's time for dinner. The rain is not so heavy now, and it's a humid, clammy evening. I go to the nearest restaurant, and I am the only diner. I sit at a table beside a huge window running almost the full length of the room. It is completely dark outside, I can see nothing. It is a bit like looking into a blank screen.

"Nobody will come tonight," the waiter remarks. "They are afraid of the lightening".

As if on cue, there's a mighty crash of thunder, the glass in the window rattles like gunfire and lightening flickers, cracking and sizzling, lighting up a castle which I didn't know was there in spectacular flashes of blue and white. I am both thrilled and alarmed by this fantastic show, and it continues as I eat my meal.

When I finally get up to leave, the waiter says it's too dangerous to walk back to the albergue, I might get hit by lightning. Even though I tell him that I've only got about three hundred yards to go, he insists anyway, and drives me to my door.

Next morning, as I cross a bridge out of the town, I decide to take a long route, as there's more than one way to

O'Cebreiro, the steepest climb of the camino. I feel fit and strong. Just a few other pilgrims are taking this route, including the two young Irish men. We walk together for a while, but they are younger and fitter than I am, so they are going to walk on. The guitarist is having trouble carrying his guitar, as the strap on the guitar case has broken, and is too short to tie it so that it fits him. I suggest we swop, he can carry my rucksack and I will carry the guitar, it is light and fits me comfortably. He carries my rucksack on his chest, in front, and pronounces it fine, so we agree to meet at the top, in O'Cebreiro. They walk away, and are soon out of sight.

This route is a testing one, but for the first few hours I enjoy the climb, not keeping track of how far I've travelled. Twice I go through a farmyard, and each time I am entreated to play the guitar, but I have to admit that I can't play it. The first family give me a beer, the second give me some juicy tomatoes. Onwards and upwards I go, very glad that I'm only carrying the guitar, wondering how the young man is doing with two packs to carry. The hours slip by, and I have lost track of time and distance. It's very hot, and I have not met any other pilgrims. I come to a makeshift bar in a ruined building, with a tent nearby if you really can't go any further. The bar is quaint, being the window sill in a piece of a wall, there is no roof, no doors, just this one wall left with its window sill. A tall, bronzed Australian is the barman. He tells me there is another seven kilometres to go.

I have slowed considerably, but I feel fine, so I plod on steadily. A man comes towards me down the narrow track, carrying a bicycle, and I move aside to let him pass. He does not speak. A little later, he passes me again, going up, this time without a bicycle. Again, he does not speak. When he appears for the third time, I start to get a bit panicky, thinking it odd that he keeps going by. I start to walk much faster, but I only succeed in making myself feel sick and dizzy. I take a long drink of water, and try to keep calm. Then, up ahead, I see another pilgrim. I hurry on to catch up, and am relieved to find a French girl, Danielle, who I met in Zubiri. I must look distressed, because she makes me stop and breathe, do some yoga, and drink more water. I obviously haven't forgotten Ponferrada. We walk on together, and it seems only minutes as we reach O'Cebreiro. There is a fiesta in full swing, and a great food market, but first things first, I go to check into the albergue. There is a long queue, and in the middle are the two Irish lads who have my rucksack. The guitarist is glad to be reunited with his guitar, but my rucksack seems really heavy after carrying the guitar. The woman at the desk scowls when she sees the guitar, making it clear that she does not approve of noise, reluctantly allowing them in. This is a clean, bright albergue, with beds, not bunks, and lots of space between each one. I have a quick shower, then it's out to enjoy the night, tiredness forgotten. The food is amazing, especially the huge loaves of bread, as round and big as a dustbin lid. There is every kind of fruit, and empanadas so big they could feed a family for a couple of days. I am ravenous after the long day's walk, and I buy a slice of an empanada and a carton of pineapple chunks in a sweet, sticky syrup.

I join a group of people I recognize, and sitting with them is the man I met earlier carrying the bicycle. He is called Alan, from Somerset in England, and he lives just a few miles from my sister. It's a small world. I ask him why he was going back and forth, and he explains that his bicycle had broken, and he was directed down to a place where he could have it repaired. The person who was able to do this needed some parts, so Alan had to go back up again to get the necessary part, then all the way down again. When it was finally ready, he still had to go up again to O'Cebreiro. He is now so tired he almost falls off the bench we are sitting on.

Never mind, it's downhill all the way to Triacastela tomorrow.

PART TWENTY-TWO

IT'S ALL GOING TOO FAST.

There seems to be more and more pilgrims every day, streaming towards Santiago. I don't want it to end, but there is an air of purpose and excitement now, and I can't help being drawn along faster than I want to go. Now there is no time for introspection, solitude is rare, as time escalates, sliding silkily along like the dark heavy waters of a deep river. I reach Monte Gozo, and I stand in the warm, white blankness of a mid-morning haze, trying not to cry. I could be in Santiago before lunchtime, but I keep thinking of the end, of not walking, of the mundane days when it's all over, and I am not ready for that yet. I decide to wait until tomorrow morning, and I sit in the sun for a while, then go to get a bed in the albergue. During the afternoon, I lie on my bunk, trying to think of what I have learned, and from whom. Have I changed? What will I remember? Have I come to a place of acceptance with God, whoever He might be? Who will I remember?

And the image that comes to me is of the pale figure of a man lifting his hand in farewell, then fading wraith-like into the night.

PART TWENTY-THREE

UNTITLED.

I pull on my boots carefully, anointing my heels and toes with the merest smear of Vaseline, as though I had many miles to go. I put on my cleanest tee-shirt, and my still damp shorts – I washed them last night, though I only have one pair. My breath is heavy and I feel shaky. Deliberately, I take a long time to do every little thing, like a reluctant child silently protesting at being taken somewhere it does not want to go. But now there is nothing more to do but walk, so I lift my stick, shrug my rucksack on my back, and take the first steps of my final day walking the Camino de Santiago de Compostela.

The mist has begun to wisp away, the air is fresh, and around me there are many other pilgrims, all a little subdued, even solemn. There is no conversation. Downhill to the busy outskirts of the city, and across busy roads, watching carefully as traffic careers madly down to each set of lights, screeching to a halt at the last minute. In no time at all, I'm lost. This, however, is a different kind of 'lost' – I wander along, outwardly calm, while inside a small knot of grief grows, knowing that soon I will have to just…. stop. No matter how I try to go slower, or take another wrong turning, I am nearing the Prazo Obradoiro where the main Cathedral entrance is.

I enter the old city under the Porto do Camino, and am absorbed into the medieval atmosphere at once. There is no traffic in the old city, and I am intrigued to find that I can hear the soft footfalls of the people thronging the streets. I hear the clinking of glasses, the rattle of cutlery, the hum and buzz of conversation from the many tables lining the streets. My feet slide occasionally on the cobbles, worn smooth over hundreds of years by thousands of pilgrims. I pass down streets with arches, colonnades, and beautiful stone work. I can't help running my hand along the walls and I imagine other pilgrims down the ages doing the same thing, linking us over the span of time.

The smell of food is tantalizing, and in a window, a lobster reposes in a large tank of water awaiting his culinary fate, lazily waving, not drowning. Tourists linger over souvenirs – jewellery, pottery, bright faux pilgrim paraphernalia. Music pours from every street, here an earnest man with kettledrums, there a pair of superior violinists tuning up. A small choir of quiet little girls giggle when the deep, earthy sound of a didgeridoo blasts out a note just as they go by. A string quartet sits on the Rua de Azabacheria, playing beautiful music, oblivious to everything around them, and I feel my heart is breaking. I try to hold back for a moment at the top of the flight of steps which sweep down into the cool, dim tunnel leading to the Prazo Obradoiro. but I am drawn along with the crowd of other pilgrims. The music fades, my breath is caught in my throat, just one more step, out into the sunlight and suddenly - it's over.

WHO IS HE, ANYWAY?

I shouted His praise to the skies,
Though I did not know Him.
I searched for Him everywhere.
I looked in all the wrong places.
I could not find Him in sermons, in making offerings,
At shrines, nor in echoing cathedrals.

He said, "If you have something against your brother, don't bring me your sacrifices.
Go, make it right with your brother, then bring your sacrifices."

Then, I found Him when He humbled me,
I found Him in the kindness of strangers,
The blessing of a smile, the stillness of the night.
He warmed me with love, absolved me by grace.
I do not know the answers to all questions,
But this I know –
Without Him, there is no me.